DYNAMIC

Text by CLYDE NEWTON

Photography by GERALD J. TOFF

Sumo

KODANSHA INTERNATIONAL
Tokyo • New York • London

木村庄之助

芝荒馬

4

Colorful *nobori* banners placed outside the arena during tournaments
list the name of every rikishi who is to compete.

The publisher wishes to thank the Sumo Association for its kind cooperation.

All Japanese names appearing in this book are given in traditional order, with surname first.

A conversion rate of one hundred yen to the U.S. dollar was used in calculations.

The illustration on page 19 is by Takumi Yamamoto and first appeared in Kodansha's
Japan: An Illustrated Encyclopedia, 1993.

The illustrations on pages 89, 91, 93 and 95 are from *Asahi Supotsu Rinji Zokan,
Ozumo Haru Basho Go*, 1952 and *Asahi Supotsu Rinji Zokan, Ozumo Aki Basho
Tenbo*, 1953.

Distributed in the United States by Kodansha America, Inc., 114 Fifth Avenue, New
York, New York 10011, and in the United Kingdom and continental Europe by
Kodansha Europe Ltd., 95 Aldwych, London WC2B 4JF.
Published by Kodansha International Ltd., 17–14 Otowa 1-chome, Bunkyo-ku, Tokyo
112, and Kodansha America, Inc.

Library of Congress Cataloging-in-Publication Data

Newton, Clyde.
    Dynamic sumo / text by Clyde Newton: photography by Gerald J. Toff.—1st ed.
        p.   cm.
    ISBN 4-7700-1802-9
    ISBN 4-7700-1963-7 (Hawaiian Edition)
    1. Sumo. 2. Sumo—Pictorial works. I. Toff, Gerald J. II. Title.
GV1197. N 45 1994
796.8'125—dc20
                                                                    94-12334
                                                                        CIP

CONTENTS

III New Legends

IV Power and Technique

V Daily Life

Preface

The past few years have seen one of the greatest changes in sumo since it was first performed—the emergence not only of strong foreign *rikishi* but also of the first foreign-born *yokozuna*.

To a certain extent this reflects the growing internationalization of Japan in a world which is becoming smaller with each passing day. However, I do not think sumo will lose the essentially Japanese spirit it has developed, the essence of *sumodo* that draws people like a magnet to the six *honbasho*, official tournaments, and the many *jungyo* exhibition bouts, annually.

Recently we have seen examples of classic Japanese architecture designated as international cultural treasures. It is our hope that people around the world will view sumo not only as part of Japan's cultural heritage, but of the heritage of all mankind.

I hope that books like *Dynamic Sumo* will help explain the essence of sumo to foreign readers and thus generate an increasing awareness and understanding of *sumodo* and the traditions that are its foundations.

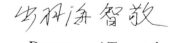

Dewanoumi Tomotaka
President (Rijicho)
Japan Sumo Association
(Nihon Sumo Kyokai)

Introduction

Sumo, Japan's *kokugi*, or unofficial "national sport," has a history spanning more than one thousand years. Its official, professional tournaments have been held regularly since the early eighteenth century.

In the 1990s, sumo has enjoyed phenomenal popularity in Japan, perhaps more than at any other stage in its history. Access to satellite television and other contemporary media throughout much of the world, combined with the rise of three powerful Hawaiian competitors, has generated an increased awareness of sumo around the world in areas including the United States, Europe and the rest of Asia. The appeal of this sport, with its fast, exciting bouts played against a backdrop of stately, elegant rituals, transcends national and cultural boundaries.

Sumo's origins are shrouded in legend. There is evidence that precursors of the sport reached Japan from the Asian mainland, most likely from China or Korea. Ancient martial arts and forms of wrestling that vaguely resemble sumo exist in many parts of the world. However, the traditions and rituals of today's professional sumo are inherently Japanese, and most closely reflect Japanese culture of the Edo period (1600–1867). Other important Japanese traditional arts such as kabuki, bunraku and Noh were also largely developed in this period.

Sumo achieved wide popularity as early as the 1780s, and managed to survive the various upheavals that have occurred in Japan over the last two hundred years. Catastrophic fires and earthquakes in the city of Edo (now Tokyo) in the eighteenth and nineteenth centuries did little more than delay the opening of tournaments by a few months. The dramatic transformation of Japan with the Meiji Restoration in 1868 brought inevitable changes to professional sumo's organization and management, but the long-standing rules of competition and rituals survived intact. The Ryogoku area of Tokyo, sumo's center since the eighteenth century, was levelled in the Great Kanto Earthquake of September 1, 1923, and again by the air raids made on Japan's capital during the Second World War, but neither of these events prevented tournaments from being held regularly.

Sumo's popularity has spiralled in the twentieth century with the development of modern communications systems such as radio and television. The sport was opened to the rest of the world in an equally dramatic sense in the 1960s with the rise of Takamiyama, a Hawaiian-born rikishi who achieved success against considerable odds. Takamiyama's dedication and perseverance won him the abiding respect not only of fans in other countries but of dyed-in-the-wool Japanese enthusiasts as well. Konishiki, Akebono and

The senior referee pours saké into the ring as part of the purification ceremony held before each tournament.

Musashimaru, all raised in Hawaii, have followed in Takamiyama's footsteps, with Akebono becoming, in January 1993, the first non-Japanese to reach sumo's highest rank, of yokozuna. The Japan Sumo Association, the organizational body overseeing the professional sport, has held official tours over the last thirty years around the globe, sparking further interest in sumo and its traditions.

The sport's colorful traditions and rituals and the dynamism of its matches are key factors in sumo's huge popularity at home and abroad. In Japan, certainly, sumo receives substantial coverage in the mass media. Most people in the country are sumo fans, or at least have a reasonable degree of interest at some points in their lives. Without a doubt, television has played an important role in awakening interest in sumo at home.

Much the same can be said of sumo's appeal to non-Japanese. If media coverage overseas can be increased, sumo has the potential to become popular worldwide, with a following in the hundreds of millions.

I first saw sumo on television in 1961, when I was five or six. I soon became curious, and wanted to know more than was evident from TV broadcasts. I had a Japanese neighbor who was studying English and we began to trade off—my old textbooks for his sumo magazines. Looking at those was what really hooked me. I have always had a keen interest in sumo's history, as well as in the more modern developments. I believe that knowledge of the history contributes greatly to understanding of the sport as it is played today.

Gerry Toff, the photographer for *Dynamic Sumo*, has spent most of the last thirty-six years in Japan. He has studied sumo extensively from the angles of a scholar and photographer, and also taken up other Japanese martial arts like stick fighting (*jojutsu*). Unlike many other sumo photographers, Gerry has tended to concentrate on capturing sumo's rituals and traditions.

Since all the sport's participants are in constant motion, photographing sumo can be extremely difficult. But Gerry Toff is a skilled photographer who has taken thousands of slides of sumo over the last fifteen years. In this book we present some of his best work.

Finally, a note on terminology. In most cases I have alternated between using Japanese terms and their English equivalents.

However, I have preferred to use Japanese consistently for several of the terms appearing most frequently in this book. Specifically, I have avoided "wrestler" (*rikishi*), "stable" (*heya*) and "grand champion" (*yokozuna*). These particular English terms have connotations which may be misleading. Having been used for years in the context of other sports, they fail to call to mind a vivid image specifically associated with sumo. Further, the trend in English writing on sumo in recent years, as the sport has become better known around the world, has been to favor these Japanese terms for their greater preciseness.

I wrote *Dynamic Sumo* to further understanding of sumo in an easily accessible, visual format. The book is intended to convey sumo's beauty and dynamism, rather than serve as a comprehensive statistical handbook.

I hope that *Dynamic Sumo* will provide readers with useful information and, just as importantly, encourage them to study in greater depth the particular aspects of sumo that hold the greatest appeal for them.

Clyde Newton
Tokyo
August, 1994

I

WHAT IS SUMO?

Sumo is distinguished from other sports by the importance it places on ritual and ceremony.

An Overview

Sumo is more than just a sport; it is also a series of time-honored rituals, a way of life and a living history.

The rules are simple enough that even a person watching for the first time can easily make sense of them. Sumo is a contest of strength, technique and agility. Bouts are often furious struggles that take just a matter of seconds. The first rikishi (a term greatly to be preferred to the English "sumo wrestler") to step out of the ring, or touch its surface with any part of his body other than the soles of his feet, loses.

The rituals preceding matches follow a set pattern repeated by all the rikishi taking part in a tournament, from those in the lowest divisions whose bouts begin the day to the highest-ranking competitors featured in the final showdown. Each match starts with a ring announcer summoning the rikishi by name onto the *dohyo*, or ring. When the competitors step into the dohyo, the referee again calls out their names. The rikishi then perform the *shikiri*, an elaborate series of rituals that takes place before each bout. Once the referee signals that the time allotted for this period is up, the two men lunge toward one another in the crucial initial charge known as the *tachi-ai*.

Shorter bouts end in five to ten seconds. Longer ones may go on for a few minutes. The heavier or stronger competitor has an advantage, but outstanding technique, superior balance and will to win are among the many factors that can compensate for lesser weight or strength. Smaller rikishi have often been known to defeat opponents twice their size, hence the unpredictability that provides much of sumo's excitement.

Unlike Japanese society in general, promotion in sumo is based on merit alone. Those who win advance in the ranks, and those who lose are demoted. With six fifteen-day tournaments every year, sumo is fiercely competitive. Rikishi must stay in top condition in order to succeed, and those who do not quickly find themselves in a downward spiral. New recruits begin their careers early, often just out of junior high shool, and few survive in active competition for more than fifteen or sixteen years.

Yet sumo's way of life and traditions do closely mirror Japanese society. Rikishi compete as individuals, but must belong to a group, known as the heya, often referred to as "sumo stables." It is within these groups that rikishi train and master techniques. Almost all, in fact, live in their heya, except some of those who have, on the basis of their higher rank, begun to draw a salary and thus are able to enjoy increased independence.

Sumo also reflects Japanese culture in that any displays of emotion on the dohyo, whether during the bout itself or the preceding rituals, are frowned upon. Etiquette is to be observed at all times. Rikishi never dispute the verdict of the referee or the judges.

Throughout the process of Japan's transformation over the last 140 years from a closed, feudal nation to an economic superpower, sumo's traditions have carried on largely unchanged. These rituals—most of which date back to the seventeenth century—continue to lend sumo an air of beauty and spectacle that sets it apart from other sports.

Dohyo—The Sumo Ring

The word *dohyo* literally means "clay and rice bales." The term was current by the end of the seventeenth century, when rings were simply marked out by packing *tawara* (straw bales, normally used to hold rice) tightly with clay and arranging them in a circle on the ground.

Today the large, three-dimensional ring which stands at the center of the sumo arena is itself formed from clay. Tawara, now carefully half-buried in the surface, trace out a circle on the top. Another ring of tawara marks off the extreme outer edges.

The dohyo rises about 1 foot 9.6 inches (fifty-five centimeters) off the ground. It is traditionally constructed from *arakida* soil, taken from the banks of the Arakawa River in Saitama Prefecture, just north of Tokyo. This soil's high clay content is ideal for helping the ring keep its shape. But arakida soil has become scarce in recent years as a result of the rapid pace of Saitama's urbanization, and dirt from Ibaraki Prefecture is now sometimes used instead.

The action takes place inside the inner circle, which measures about fifteen feet (4.6 meters) in diameter. The tawara placed at each of the four cardinal points is set back a few inches from the circle proper. These four spots are called *tokudawara*, or special rice bales, and are the only places where a step outside the ring is not considered a loss.

Several tawara sunk at regular intervals into each side of the ring serve as the steps, or *fumidawara*, used for climbing in and out.

In theory, the entire dohyo is reconstructed for each tournament. The dohyo is, indeed, completely rebuilt for each official tournament held in cities other than Tokyo, since these are not frequent enough to justify keeping the ring up year round. But in Tokyo the ring stays up, with only the top third or so replaced between uses. The dimensions of the dohyo used in the many additional regional exhibitions held throughout the year are identical. But here, since the time available for construction is usually limited, a specially constructed frame is often used as the base.

The completed dohyo is purified in a Shinto-style ceremony known as the *dohyo matsuri*. A top *gyoji* (referee) officiates, dressed in the white robe of a Shinto priest. Offerings of chestnuts, kelp and cuttlefish are placed deep inside the ring and prayers are offered for the safety of the rikishi competing in the upcoming tournament. An abbreviated version of the ceremony is held even for exhibition matches.

Over the ring hangs the *yakata*, a roof which is slightly smaller than the dohyo and suspended from the ceiling of the Kokugikan or other arenas where honbasho are held. Though it weighs many tons, this roof can be taken away from the dohyo area when the building is used for events other than sumo. A curtain, the *mizuhiki-maku*, hangs from the eaves of the yakata, and is emblazoned with crests showing the emblem of the Sumo Association. The four pillars that supported the yakata in earlier years have been replaced with black, white, red and green tassels that hang down from each corner of the roof.

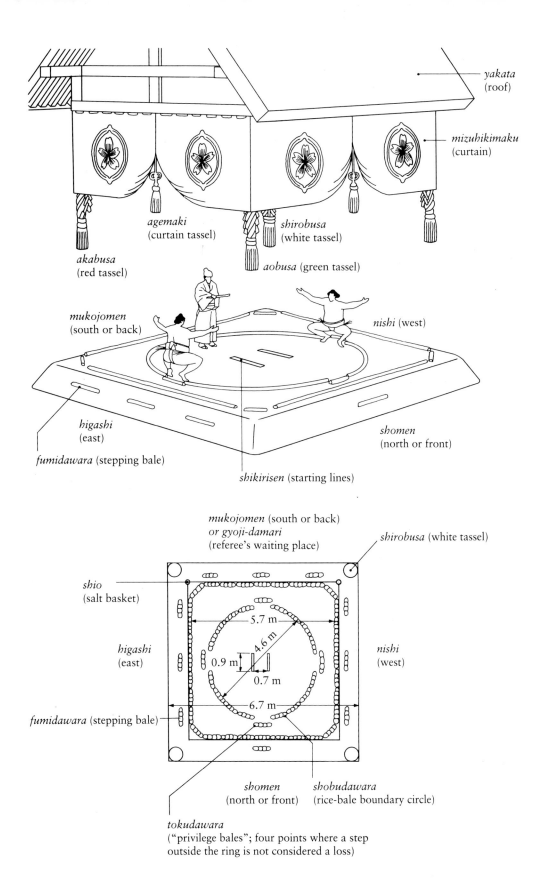

yakata
(roof)

mizuhikimaku
(curtain)

agemaki
(curtain tassel)

shirobusa
(white tassel)

akabusa
(red tassel)

aobusa (green tassel)

mukojomen
(south or back)

nishi (west)

higashi
(east)

shomen
(north or front)

fumidawara (stepping bale)

shikirisen (starting lines)

mukojomen (south or back)
or gyoji-damari
(referee's waiting place)

shirobusa (white tassel)

shio
(salt basket)

5.7 m

4.6 m

0.9 m

0.7 m

6.7 m

higashi
(east)

nishi
(west)

fumidawara (stepping bale)

shomen
(north or front)

shobudawara
(rice-bale boundary circle)

tokudawara
("privilege bales"; four points where a step
outside the ring is not considered a loss)

Sumo Dohyo

Banzuke—The Official Ranking Sheet

The *banzuke* is the official sumo ranking sheet published prior to each of the six annual tournaments. With the exception of the banzuke for the Hatsu Basho in January, which must be released before the New Year's holidays, the banzuke is issued on the Monday thirteen days before the start of each basho.

Though priced at just fifty yen (about half the price of a candy bar), the banzuke is a work of art. The name of every rikishi, referee, elder and top-ranking yobidashi—a total of more than one thousand men at present—is listed on this sheet measuring just 21 by 15 inches (53 by 39 centimeters). The order of new rankings is first drafted by the judges, usually on the Wednesday after a tournament ends. Then the actual work of writing out the banzuke is done by two high-ranking referees.

Since all new rankings are confidential until their official release, the referees involved spend up to ten days sequestered at home producing the new banzuke. The original is written with a calligraphy brush on a single large sheet of paper. This is then printed professionally on *washi,* or traditional Japanese paper, one-fourth that size. Newly-printed banzuke are provided to everyone listed on it, and to others in the sumo world, for distribution to patrons, relatives and friends. The Sumo Association also sells a limited number to the general public at the Kokugikan before and during tournaments.

The names of the rikishi are arranged on the banzuke in order of ranking, splitting those of the same rank into two sides—the east (or *higashi,* listed on the right-hand side of the sheet) and west (*nishi,* shown on the left). This system of arrangement dates back to the eighteenth century. The east has traditionally been considered somewhat more prestigious than the west.

The ranking sheet is T-shaped because of the presence of competitors known as *haridashi* at the four highest ranks. In theory, a maximum of two rikishi are to be named to each of these ranks, but in fact there are sometimes more. When this happens, an "additional," or haridashi, section must be created for that rank. The additional rikishi are listed on the portion of the banzuke which juts out at either side of the top to form the "T."

Young rikishi from each heya pick up copies of the new ranking sheet from the Sumo Association.

Like much of Japanese society, sumo has an intricate hierarchy, but here promotion is based on performance alone, and not on age or length of service. Rikishi are promoted for *kachikoshi*, or winning records. A winning record corresponds to four or more of the seven bouts held between unsalaried rikishi, and eight or more of the fifteen fought by those of the salaried ranks.

The following are sumo's rankings:

THE UNSALARIED RANKS

■ *Maezumo* Unranked beginners.

■ *Jonokuchi* The lowest-ranked division, to which all newcomers are promoted in their second tournament. The jonokuchi now has about sixty rikishi on each of the higashi (east) and nishi (west) sides, for a total of about 120.

■ *Jonidan* Sumo's largest division, with over two hundred rikishi on either side. In the lower part of the division, even a losing record may result in promotion, as in the jonokuchi.

■ *Sandanme* A total of one hundred rikishi on the two sides of the banzuke. Less than half of all newcomers to sumo will ever get beyond the sandanme. Promotion and demotion can be drastic—a 4–3 record can result in promotion by 10 or more ranks, while a 3–4 record can mean being sent back 10–15 ranks.

■ *Makushita* This is the highest unsalaried division. It is very hard for any but the strongest rikishi to get beyond this rank (the name of which literally means "below the curtain" and suggests the great distance between this and the next-highest step).

THE SALARIED RANKS

■ *Juryo* The lowest salaried level. Rikishi at this level are full-fledged *sekitori* (salaried rikishi) with their own *tsukebito*, or attendants. Current sumo rules allow for a total of just twenty-six juryo rikishi—thirteen on each side of the banzuke.

The makuuchi (the top division) is subdivided as follows:

■ *Maegashira* Rank-and-file makuuchi rikishi. Fifteen or sixteen men on each side of the banzuke, for a total of about thirty.

The *sanyaku* is composed of the makuuchi's four highest ranks:

■ *Komusubi* The lowest sanyaku rank. Status and salary are equivalent to those of the sekiwake.

■ *Sekiwake* The second sanyaku rank. The stepping-board to ozeki promotion, and the rank to which demoted ozeki are sent back.

■ *Ozeki* Sumo's second-highest rank, this was the highest rank until that of yokozuna was created in 1890. Only one in about three hundred rikishi reaches ozeki. Ozeki are demoted only if they turn in *makekoshi* (losing records—that is, a greater number of losses than wins) in two consecutive tournaments.

■ *Yokozuna* Sumo's highest rank, achieved by an average of about one in five hundred new rikishi. Yokozuna cannot be demoted. They are simply expected to retire if their performance falls below expectations.

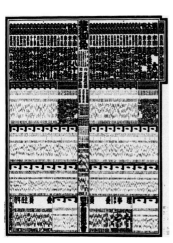

The official ranking sheet, or *banzuke*

Akebono and his master, Azu-mazeki, look over the first banzuke on which Akebono appears as a yokozuna.

Gyoji and *Shinpan*—Referees and Judges

Bouts are monitored by a single referee who moves about the ring throughout the match, and a number of judges stationed around it. In other words, officials view every bout from many different angles, which helps ensure accuracy and fairness.

GYOJI

Gyoji are specialists who devote their entire working careers to the profession. Like rikishi, all belong to a specific heya, which most enter at the age of fifteen or sixteen, fresh out of junior high. And gyoji, like the competitors themselves, are ranked.

Sumo Association rules fix the number of chief referees (*tategyoji*) at two. The road to the top of the profession is very long. Promotion to *juryo-kaku*, or qualification to referee matches between those at the lowest salaried rank, requires about fifteen years. Yet another fifteen years, on average, will pass before a referee attains *makuuchi-kaku*. The tategyoji typically has forty or fifty years of experience. In most cases, his tenure is fairly brief, since the profession has a mandatory retirement age of sixty-five.

Gyoji are promoted mainly on the basis of seniority. However, accuracy in refereeing is also a critical factor in advancement. A large number of *sashichi-gai*, or decisions overturned by the judges, hinders promotion. Other factors taken into consideration are good voice projection, leadership qualities, calligraphic skills and the speed and agility essential for getting around the dohyo quickly enough to be able to reach accurate decisions.

Senior gyoji are expected to pass down the traditions and skills of the profession to their juniors. A gyoji's responsibilities extend beyond the dohyo and include, for instance, preparing the banzuke as well as the washi paper placards which are hung outside the Kokugikan to publicize the day's makuuchi bouts. Referees also help out in their heya, sometimes serving as secretaries.

The gyoji's most essential function, of course, is refereeing. On each day of a tournament, the lowest-ranking gyoji officiates at up to ten bouts, while the higher of the two tategyoji officiates at only the final match.

All gyoji take either Kimura or Shikimori as their unofficial "family names." These are the two traditional refereeing names that have existed since the early eighteenth century. Referees' names, like those of rikishi, can be changed; the same gyoji's name may change even back and forth between Kimura and Shikimori. The senior tategyoji is always called Kimura Shono-suke, while the name given to the second-ranked of the top referees is Shiki-mori Inosuke.

SHINPAN

Shinpan are all retired rikishi who have remained in sumo as elders, or *oyakata*. Shinpan generally come up for reelection every two years. The total number of judges is fixed at twenty, with a set proportion of these allotted to each *ichimon*, or group of heya.

Any former rikishi who has elder status is theoretically eligible to become a shinpan. In practice, most will have reached at least a high maegashira rank during their careers in the ring.

Three head or deputy head judges (*shinpan bucho* or *fukubucho*) are also appointed, and it is their responsibility to head the judging panels for bouts in sumo's two top divisions, the makuuchi and juryo. In recent years, all shinpan bucho and fukubucho have been former yokozuna.

All bouts are supervised by five judges, stationed around the ring, with two being placed on the south side. One of those on the south serves as *tokei-gakari*, or timekeeper; it is his responsibility to determine when the shikiri should conclude and the bout begin.

The judges monitor the tachi-ai carefully, and stop the match if either riki-

Above: A bout early in the day. This lower-ranked referee's status is obvious from his bare feet. At left: The then second-ranked referee, the late 26th Shikimori Inosuke.

The *mono-ii*. After a particularly close match, the judges may gather in the ring to reconsider the referee's decision.

shi does not rise properly.

In addition, any one of the judges has the right to challenge a decision made by the gyoji. When this happens, the shinpan gather within the ring itself for a *mono-ii*, or conference. The judges have three options, which they choose among by majority vote. The first is to accept the gyoji's verdict; the second, to declare a *sashichigai*, or complete reversal of the decision; and the third to decide that the fight was too close to call, and order a *torinaoshi*, or rematch.

Still another shinpan bucho or fukubucho watches all juryo and makuuchi matches on closed circuit television in a separate room, relaying his opinions by headset to the judges beside the dohyo.

The shinpan stationed on the ring's north side acts as spokesman, announcing the result of any mono-ii over a public-address system. In matches of the juryo or makuuchi divisions, the shinpan bucho or fukubucho takes this role.

Honbasho—Official Tournaments

Honbasho are held six times a year. The January, May and September tournaments are held in Tokyo at the Kokugikan. The March tournament is held at the Osaka Municipal Gymnasium, the July tournament in Nagoya's Aichi Prefectural Gymnasium and the November tournament at the Fukuoka International Center.

The January tournament, or Hatsu Basho, dates back to the eighteenth century. January and February are the coldest months of the year in Tokyo, yet it was possible to hold this tournament in the open air in the days before the first sumo stadium was built, since there is little rain in the capital in January. The Hatsu Basho usually opens on the second Sunday in January, after the long New Year's holidays are over and business has returned to normal.

The Osaka tournament in March is referred to as the Haru Basho, or spring tournament. Prior to 1953, when this tournament was established, the January event in Tokyo was known as the Haru Basho (though Tokyo is far from springlike at that time of year). Perhaps partly because the early spring weather is very changeable, the Osaka tournament tends to be unpredictable. There have been many upset winners of the makuuchi championship at Osaka in the last thirty years.

The Natsu Basho, or summer tournament, is held at the Kokugikan in May. This usually begins shortly after the end of the Golden Week holidays which run through May 5. Until 1944, the Natsu Basho and the Hatsu (at

On the first day of each official tournament, the president of the Sumo Association, accompanied by all the sanyaku rikishi, addresses the audience.

that time, Haru) Basho in January were the only tournaments held in most years.

The Nagoya Basho starts at the beginning of July. Less training time elapses between the May and July tournaments than between any other two. This tournament is always scheduled to start early in the month, in order to allow as much time as possible for the regional exhibition tours held afterwards. Some rikishi are better able than others to handle the summer heat, and this tournament's outcome, like that of the Osaka basho, is often surprising.

The Aki Basho, or autumn tournament, has been held in Tokyo in September—in the midst of the typhoon season—since 1953. An autumn tournament was in fact first added to the yearly schedule in 1944, but at that time the event was held on a more variable schedule, at some point between September and November.

The Kyushu Basho has been held in Fukuoka each November since 1957. In the 1980s this tournament offered little by way of suspense, since Chiyonofuji won the championship there every year from 1981–88.

The number of days in each honbasho has changed many times over sumo's history, but since 1949 has stood at fifteen. All tournaments begin and end on Sundays. The day's matches begin at about nine or ten A.M., and all ceremonies are scheduled to conclude at six in the evening.

Dohyo-iri—The Ring-Entering Ceremony

A typical day at a honbasho gets underway at nine o'clock in the morning. Only a few die-hard fans are on hand to watch the bouts between the rikishi ranked in the jonokuchi, the lowest division. Matches in this and the next-highest division, the jonidan, tend to end very quickly. One reason for this is the very short time limit placed in the lower divisions on the *shikiri*, the elaborate series of rituals that precedes each bout. Another is that rikishi at this level tend to have few sophisticated techniques at their disposal, so that wins are generally achieved straightforwardly.

The audience is still quite sparse during the jonidan and sandanme bouts. Matches between rikishi ranked at the makushita, the highest unsalaried level, do not start until one-thirty or two in the afternoon. Five bouts before the end of the makushita competition, the first *dohyo-iri*, or ring-entering ceremony —that of the juryo rikishi—takes place.

All those holding this rank file into the ring, dressed in the lavish decorative aprons known as *keshomawashi*. They arrange themselves around the outer diameter, looking out toward the audience, until the last man enters, when all turn in to face the ring. Finally they clap hands, raise their keshomawashi slightly, and throw up their arms.

They leave in the same order in which they entered—by ascending order of their ranking on the banzuke. After a brief interval, the last five makushita bouts follow, and the juryo matches begin.

The next dohyo-iri comes after all the juryo bouts are over. This ring-entering ceremony involves all the makuuchi rikishi except the yokozuna, and is performed in precisely the same way as was the juryo's.

This is immediately followed by individual dohyo-iri performed by each current yokozuna. After an intermission lasting ten minutes or so, during which the next day's bouts are announced, the makuuchi bouts start, at about four-thirty in the afternoon.

Rikishi wait for the last man to step up during the ring-entering ceremony (*makuuchi dohyo-iri*).

Shikiri—Pre-Bout Rituals

Rikishi of every division go through a preliminary ritual known as the *shikiri* before beginning their bouts. Sumo Association rules stipulate that, at the unsalaried ranks, these rituals be kept down to two minutes. The time limit for the shikiri of matches at the juryo level is three minutes, and for those of the makuuchi, four.

Rikishi come out and sit in front of the dohyo two bouts before their own begins. They are called onto the dohyo proper by the *yobidashi*, or ring announcer, when the time arrives for their match. After stepping up into the ring, they launch not into the fight, but into the shikiri.

First, each rikishi stamps his legs twice in his corner of the ring. He then rinses out his mouth with *chikaramizu* (literally, "strength water"), and wipes his mouth and upper body with a sheet of *chikaragami* ("strength paper"). He then goes over to the tokudawara closest to his corner and, squatting there, claps once, then stretches out his arms and turns them palm-upward. This sequence of the ritual, known as *chiri-chozu*, has ancient origins, and symbolizes that the rikishi is unarmed.

The rikishi then retreat to their corners, and emerge throwing salt—considered a purifying agent—onto the ring. Each squats behind the *shikiri-sen*, or starting lines from behind which they make the initial charge. The two lock eyes for a time, then rise, in many cases pausing to give each other one more long look before going back to their corners again. The rikishi repeat this part of the ritual several times.

The entire sequence may seem unnecessarily time-consuming to the new viewer of sumo, but in fact the time spent on the shikiri is essential. Each man uses it to size up and try to intimidate his opponent. This opportunity to gauge the other's frame of mind helps the rikishi perform a proper initial charge. The shikiri also serves to build audience tension—an important function, especially given that matches may end in a matter of seconds.

The shikiri is, for all intents and purposes, part of the bout.

Tachi-ai—The Initial Clash

Until the beginning of the Showa period (1926–89), there were no limits as to how long the shikiri could go on. In some cases it would continue for thirty minutes or even an hour. Once, in the 1860s, two makuuchi rikishi performed an apparently endless shikiri that seems to have worn them both out: it was followed by more than one hundred false starts, and the bout was declared a draw before they could manage a successful tachi-ai.

Sumo's rules state that both rikishi must place at least one hand, and preferably both, on the shikiri-sen before launching their tachi-ai. The judge assigned to act as timekeeper signals the referee when the shikiri is to end and the match begin. Each rikishi is offered a towel when he returns to his corner for the last time. The referee then calls out the phrase, *"seigen jikan ippai"* ("time is up"). When the two return and square off once more, the gyoji lowers his *gunbai* (literally, "war fan"; in fact a lacquered wooden board decorated with a long tassel) in front of them, indicating that they are now to launch their charge toward one another.

Rikishi who fail to develop a strong tachi-ai are usually at a disadvantage.

Above: The ring announcer calls the next two competitors onto the ring for their bout. Above right: The referee also calls out the name of each rikishi, while pointing his fan toward their respective sides. Right: Rinsing out the mouth with the "strength water" thought to purify and bring good luck. Below: The *chiri-chozu*, a symbolic gesture showing that the rikishi have no weapons.

The *shikiri* begins with the riki-shi being summoned onto the dohyo by the yobidashi. Each man stamps his feet while standing in his corner, then emerges throwing salt onto the ring.

The two then squat behind their respective starting lines.

After standing and glaring at one another, the rikishi go back again from the center to their sides, to repeat the entire ritual.

Seigen jikan ippai! Time's up! The referee lowers his fan to indicate that the match is to begin.

The *tachi-ai*, or initial clash

At the end of a bout, the referee points toward the winner's side.

However, in recent years, some smaller rikishi like Mainoumi and Tomono-hana have compensated by adopting unorthodox but acceptable tachi-ai—jumping out quickly from behind the shikiri-sen, for instance, in hopes of confusing a larger, slower opponent.

Kensho—Cash Awards

Sumo bouts are usually over in less than a minute, sometimes in less than a second. Matches have gotten noticeably shorter since the 1940s, and nowadays even the largest rikishi can be remarkably fast.

As mentioned earlier, a bout is won when either of the contestants steps out of the dohyo's inner circle, or when any part of his body other than the soles of his feet touch down inside the dohyo.

At the end of a match, the gyoji points his gunbai toward the winner's corner. He must do this even if both rikishi fall at the same moment, making it virtually impossible to determine a winner. But the shinpan can dispute the gyoji's call and request a mono-ii, or conference among the judges.

The vast majority of bouts, however, are won decisively. Both winner and loser return to their corners to bow to one another, and the loser leaves the ring.

Kensho banners carried around the ring before the start of each match

Here the winner of the final bout of the day accepts prize money from the chief referee.

The winner then squats in front of the gyoji and first makes a gesture of thanks with one hand, then accepts any *kensho* that may come with the win.

A kensho is a cash award of sixty thousand yen (about six hundred dollars) put up by a sponsor against a specific makuuchi bout. The victor actually receives half the award money. The rest is withheld for taxation and pension contributions toward retirement allowances.

Bouts between maegashira usually have just one or two kensho, while sanyaku matches may have as many as ten or twenty. The average number of kensho awarded for a single match rose during Japan's "bubble economy" in the late 1980s and fell heavily during the subsequent recession. On the other hand, sumo has enjoyed unprecedented popularity amid the economic downturn.

The ring-entering ceremony, as it is performed when the emperor is present at a tournament. Instead of arranging themselves in a circle as usual, the rikishi all face the imperial box, ensuring that no one's back is ever turned on the emperor.

Kokugikan—The Sumo Arena

Until 1909, all sumo tournaments were held in the open air, with rikishi at the mercy of the elements. The first plans to build an indoor sumo arena (in Hibiya Park in central Tokyo) were conceived as early as 1889. But these fell through when the Sumo Association failed to obtain the necessary loan.

At the turn of the century, Ikazuchi Oyakata (the former yokozuna Umegatani I), at that time the head of the Sumo Association, used his connections and reputation to give the project the impetus needed for completion. When officials of the Kawasaki Bank asked Ikazuchi what collateral he could offer for the large sums he wanted to borrow, he is said to have rolled up his sleeves, baring his muscular arms. He got the loan.

Ground was broken in 1907 for the first covered stadium ever designed for sumo tournaments, within the compound of the Eko-in, a temple located in Tokyo's Ryogoku and the site of most basho held in the area for more than a century. Japan's construction technology may be world-class today, but was still in its infancy at that time. Thus, the Kokugikan took about three years to construct, although it was a fairly simple wood and brick structure with a steel frame. Upon its completion in 1909 it immediately became one of the city's great landmarks. Its domed ceiling nearly one hundred feet (30.5 meters) high made it one of Tokyo's tallest buildings, visible from several miles away.

The building was first named the Josetsukan ("permanent hall"). Its opening coincided with the peak years of the so-called Ume-Hitachi era of yokozuna Umegatani II and Hitachiyama, and helped to bring about a sumo boom.

The Josetsukan was soon renamed the Kokugikan, or "hall of the national sport." Other cities, envious of this honor, quickly erected their own kokugikans. The Kyoto and Osaka sumo associations built similar arenas, as did Toyama Prefecture, the Higo area in Kyushu, the city of Nagoya and even the Asakusa area of Tokyo just across the Sumida River from Ryogoku. The Osaka and Kyoto kokugikans were used chiefly for sumo for a time, but some of the other imitators were soon turned into theaters.

The first Tokyo Kokugikan had a brief life span. Between honbasho it was rented out for various exhibitions, and during a doll show in November 1917, it caught fire and burned to the ground. No one was killed, but the Sumo Kyokai was uninsured and, to make matters worse, obliged to pay for damage to the adjoining Eko-in temple complex.

The Tokyo Sumo Kyokai had no choice but temporarily to stage open-air honbasho again. The venue was changed to Yasukuni Jinja, the shrine dedicated to the war dead. Reconstruction began in 1918.

The Kokugikan was rebuilt much more sturdily, with a reinforced concrete shell capable of withstanding strong earthquakes. It was completed in the remarkably short space of just over a year, and dedicated in January 1920. Its four floors gave it a maximum capacity of about fifteen thousand people, several thousand more than the original had had.

Like the first Kokugikan, the second was a circular dome showing little influence of traditional Japanese architecture. Its increased seating capacity was achieved at the expense of comfort; by today's standards, it was quite cramped.

Yokozuna Onishiki (left) and Otori (right) square off for a bout at Yasukuni Shrine circa 1919. The shrine temporarily became the site of official tournaments while reconstruction proceeded on the first Kokugikan, destroyed in a 1917 fire.

This arena withstood the the Great Kanto Earthquake that struck three years after it opened, but was gutted in the fires, sparked by the tremor, that raced through the Ryogoku area just afterward. Most of the records of the Tokyo Sumo Association were consumed in the blaze. Despite this extensive damage, reconstruction work was completed as early as the following spring.

The refurbished building had its heyday in the 1930s with the rise of the great yokozuna Futabayama. Sumo's popularity in the Futabayama era has been matched since only by the boom set off by the young brothers Wakanohana and Takanohana in the early 1990s. The sport's tremendous popularity drew in large numbers of new recruits, so that by 1940 bouts began as early as two o'clock in the morning, and finished only about seven in the evening. Tickets to tournaments at the Kokugikan were as hard to get, in the late thirties and early forties, as they have been in recent years.

The building was gutted once again in the Great Tokyo Air Raid of March 10–11, 1945. The Sumo Association conducted hasty repairs immediately after the war ended, only to have the occupation forces expropriate the structure.

Construction began on a third Kokugikan at Kuramae, across the Sumida River from Ryogoku, in 1949. The building operated for a few years as a rather flimsy structure that had been thrown together hastily, but the economic boom that came with the Korean War enabled the Sumo Association to reinforce it with steel and concrete. A grand opening was held in September 1954 for the new Kuramae Kokugikan.

Despite the arena's relocation to Kuramae, most of sumo's heya remained in the Ryogoku area. Honbasho were held at Kuramae for thirty-five years, but no heya had an address in Kuramae during those years.

The Sumo Kyokai installed heating and air conditioning at Kuramae in 1971, but the arena was outdated by the early eighties. The association sold the site to the metropolitan government for use as a sewage treatment plant,

A view of the first Kokugikan in Ryogoku

The present Kokugikan, construction of which was completed in 1985

and purchased a former railway depot from Japan National Railways. The new plot of land was adjacent to Ryogoku Station and just a few minutes' walk from the old Ryogoku Kokugikan.

The construction of the fourth Kokugikan—the third at Ryogoku—coincided with the demolition of the second, which had stood for more than sixty years. The last honbasho was held at Kuramae in September 1984, and tournaments moved back to Ryogoku in January 1985.

This arena is the one used today. An impressive structure, it has a 150-foot (forty-seven meter) ceiling and comfortable seating. It was built to withstand the strongest earthquakes imaginable, and is meant to serve as a local evacuation center in the event of major fires, earthquakes, typhoons or other disasters. Like the previous Kokugikan it can be rented out for events other than sumo, such as boxing, pro wrestling or concerts.

The current Kokugikan also houses the offices of the Sumo Kyokai, the

Sumo Museum, the Sumo Clinic and other facilities. A retractable floor allows the dohyo to be lowered into the basement between tournaments, and the front half of the first floor's *masu-seki* (box seats) can easily be removed and reassembled at short notice. The box seats have been enlarged to accommodate the substantial increases, since the war, in the height and weight of the average Japanese. The masu-seki may be a little cramped, but remain very popular for their link to tradition and their relaxed atmosphere.

II

BEAUTY & TRADITION

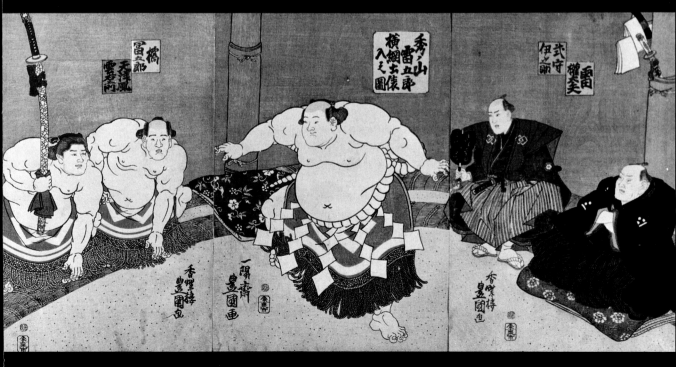

The Beauty of Sumo

Sumo's solemn, ritualized beauty gives it an unusual appeal. Without its colorful ceremonies, sumo would be just another sport, and might not have survived intact for so many centuries.

Virtually every element contributing to the sport's beauty is rooted in tradition. One of the most striking of these is the rikishi's *mage*, or topknot.

Mage—The Rikishi's Topknot

Japanese men wore their hair in a topknot for hundreds of years, beginning in the early twelfth century with the rise of a ruling class of samurai who originated the style. But in 1870, with the wave of Westernization that swept the country, the new Meiji government issued a decree ordering Japanese men—with the exception of those in sumo—to cut their mage.

The *chonmage*, an informal topknot, resembles the style popular throughout Japan during the late Edo period. Unsalaried rikishi almost always wear their hair in this style.

The higher-ranking, salaried rikishi wear this simple topknot on a day-to-day basis, and the more elaborate *oichomage* on formal occasions, including tournaments. The more structured topknot evolved only in the late nineteenth and early twentieth centuries. Sumo's *tokoyama*, or hairdressers, are specialists who usually undergo about ten years of training before completely mastering this style.

The mage, in both its forms, has now become symbolic of sumo in general.

A sumo hairdresser redoes Wakashoyo's hair in the dressing room after a bout.

Today it is the main thing that makes a rikishi stand out in a crowd, no matter what his weight or height

Keshomawashi—Colorful, Decorative Aprons

Sekitori in the juryo and makuuchi wear heavy ceremonial aprons known as keshomawashi when performing the ring-entering ceremony.

The ornate, hand-embroidered aprons are presented to sekitori by patrons comprising mainly corporations and citizens' groups from the rikishi's hometown. Keshomawashi are made from the finest quality silk or satin decorated with embroidery that requires a month or more to complete. Their most common patterns are corporate logos, calligraphy and natural scenery from the rikishi's birthplace.

Upon the announcement of their promotion to the rank of juryo, most rikishi receive just one or two keshomawashi, but those who reach ozeki or yokozuna may by that time own more than thirty. Each apron weighs about fifteen–seventeen pounds (seven–eight kilograms). Their hand-embroidery makes them very expensive to produce. A single keshomawashi costs from one million yen (ten thousand dollars) to ten or twenty times that amount.

These aprons help make the dohyo-iri a blaze of color, and watching it a highlight of a day at a sumo tournament.

The *keshomawashi*, hand-embroidered with elaborate and colorful patterns

Yokozuna Dohyo-iri—The Yokozuna Ring-Entering Ceremony

Each yokozuna performs the dohyo-iri individually, with a *tsuna*, or thick, white rope tied around his waist over his keshomawashi. The tsuna may be worn only by yokozuna on ceremonial occasions, and thus symbolizes the sport's highest rank.

In the ring-entering ceremony, the yokozuna is flanked by two attendants—the *tachimochi*, who carries his sword, and the *tsuyuharai*, or second. Rikishi chosen for these roles are almost always ranked between maegashira and sekiwake, though on rare occasions yokozuna have used ozeki as their sword-bearers.

There are two types of yokozuna dohyo-iri, Unryu-gata and Shiranui-gata, named after the two Edo-period yokozuna said to have originated the respective ceremonies. Differences between the two styles are minor. The Unryu-gata is considered "defensive," perhaps because the yokozuna stretches out just

Above, a tsuna tied in the Unryu style. At right, the Shiranui style, with two loops.

Akebono performs the yokozuna dohyo-iri at the Grand Shrine at Ise.

one arm and cups the other around his upper body when he rises slowly during the middle of the rite. In the Shiranui-gata, described as "offensive," the yokozuna stretches both arms out wide. Another distinction is that the rope-like tsuna worn by the Unryu-gata yokozuna is tied with only one loop, while the Shiranui-gata type has two.

Although there are only two types of dohyo-iri, each yokozuna performs the dohyo-iri at a different tempo, which adds variety and helps to build audience expectation. Kashiwado, a popular figure from the 1960s, often took about three minutes with his dohyo-iri, while Kitanoumi, in the 1970s and early 1980s, would often complete his in little more than one minute.

Mawashi—The Rikishi's Belt

The distance between the makushita, the highest unsalaried division, and the juryo, the lowest of the salaried ranks, is said to be akin to that separating heaven and hell. The difference is heightened by the quality of the *mawashi*, or sumo belts, used by the men competing in these neighboring divisions.

Belts used in the makushita and lower rankings are made of cotton, and cost only about ten thousand yen (one hundred dollars). Salaried rikishi, on the other hand, wear belts known as *shimekomi*, made from high-grade silk. Traditionally, shimekomi were black or dark blue, but these days almost any color is acceptable. The smallest rikishi's belt needs to be between nineteen and twenty-three feet (six–seven meters) long, while those of giants like Akebono and Konishiki require about twice that. Shimekomi are heavy, usually weighing between about thirteen and twenty-two pounds (six–ten kilograms). Since they cannot be dry-cleaned or soaked in water, most wear out within three or four years at most. Like keshomawashi, they are given to sekitori by patrons.

Shozoku—The Referee's Costume

Gyoji, or referees, are clad in brightly-colored *shozoku*, a style derived from a form of court dress worn in the Heian period (794–1185). They add to this the lacquered black hat, or *eboshi*, a modified form of a cap popular at the ancient court. The shozoku worn by gyoji in tournaments in the winter months tend to feature darker colors than do those worn in summer.

All gyoji, regardless of their ranking, wear shozoku. The costumes worn by the referees qualified to judge juryo and makuuchi bouts are nearly as costly as keshomawashi. And like the decorative aprons worn by the rikishi, referees' costumes are often gifts from patrons.

Close-up views of the top-ranking referee during the yokozuna dohyo-iri (above) and the last bout of the day (at right).

Yumitori-shiki—The Bow-Twirling Ceremony

The *yumitori-shiki*, a ceremony that follows the last bout held on each day of both official and exhibition tournaments, is generally said to have originated in the sixteenth century. It is certain that nearly two hundred years later Tanikaze, the greatest yokozuna of his time, was presented with a bow by shogun Tokugawa Ienari at a special sumo exhibition performed in the ruler's presence. Tanikaze twirled the bow on the dohyo, and the ceremony has been retained ever since.

Since January 1952, this ceremony has closed each day of every official tournament. Rikishi who perform the yumitori-shiki are usually ranked at makushita or below, and from the heya of a current yokozuna.

Rikishi assigned this role are said to be among the less promising; few have gone beyond the juryo. However, Tomoefuji, who performed the ceremony in 1989–90, has gone as far as komusubi.

The bow-twirling ceremony that closes each day of official tournaments and regional tours

The History of Sumo

The Earliest Days

No one knows just where or when sumo originated. There is some evidence that it may have travelled through China, Korea and perhaps Mongolia before reaching Japan. Sumo's history can be traced back at least 1,300 years, and perhaps more than two thousand years, in Japan.

Myths related in some of the oldest written documents focus on the sport. The oldest extant chronicle, the eighth century *Kojiki*, describes a bout between two gods, Takemikazuchi and Takeminakata. Takemikazuchi—the legendary predecessor of the imperial clan which ordered the writing of the *Kojiki* soon after coming to power—is described as having won, which doubtless helped confirm the legitimacy of that clan's rule. Another mythical bout, described in the *Nihon Shoki*, was said to have taken place between Nominosukune and Taimanokehaya in 23 B.C. The victor, Nominosukune, is credited with founding the sport at that early date. The sumo recounted in myth was often a fierce contest, continuing until one contestant was killed or incapacitated.

Sumo tournaments were held at the imperial court as early as the seventh-century reign of Empress Kogyoku. By the eighth century, just before the beginning of the Heian period (794–1185), sumo festivals known as *sumai no sechi-e* held at the Imperial Palace were regularly drawing the best rikishi to the capital from throughout the country. These festivals marked the first large-scale sumo tournaments ever held. Largely religious in nature, they centered around prayers for the nation's prosperity. There was no dohyo at the time, but rules gradually developed as sumo began to flourish.

Sumo remained popular during the Kamakura period (1185–1392), when it was first used as a martial art by the warrior class. Though sumo was less popular in the capital and with the ruling class of lords during the Ashikaga period (1338–1568), warriors and ordinary people in the regions continued to practice the sport.

Contests sponsored by the great warlord Oda Nobunaga toward the end of the sixteenth century were the first to feature sumo performed inside a ring. Rules were adopted on an *ad hoc* basis over the ensuing decades. Given the strict social controls imposed by the Tokugawa shogunate, sumo became an important means of entertaining a potentially restless public.

The Rise of the First Great Rikishi During the Edo Period

Professional sumo began early in the Edo period (1600–1867) with *kanjin-sumo*, or charity tournaments. Soon most of the proceeds from such events began to go toward maintaining a permanent group of strong competitors.

These bands of professionals formed sumo organizations in the cities of Edo (now Tokyo), Kyoto and Osaka. The first *banzuke* were drawn on wooden plaques in the final years of the seventeenth century. By the 1720s and 1730s, sumo was thriving in Kyoto and Osaka. During the next two decades tournaments also came to be held on a regular basis in Edo.

Tanikaze Kajinosuke, professional sumo's first great rikishi, made his

A rendering of a sumo bout between two mythical figures said to have taken place in 23 B.C. Collection of the Sumo Museum.

This painting depicts the type of large-scale tournament first held at the Imperial Palace in the eighth century. Collection of the Sumo Museum.

debut in 1769. He and rival Onogawa—the first rikishi ever named to the highest rank, of yokozuna, during his own lifetime—were the central figures in this "golden age" of the sport. Prints featuring rikishi were made and sold by the *ukiyo-e* woodblock artists of the time, and were to fade in popularity only with the introduction of picture postcards at the turn of the twentieth century.

Tanikaze was a giant for his time, standing about six foot two inches (1.89 meters) and weighing about 363 pounds (165 kilograms). But eighteenth-century professionals were a far cry from the hulking figures who now dominate the sport. Many would have been shorter than today's average Japanese.

In addition, many rikishi began their careers at the age of twenty or later, and competed for a good twenty or thirty years. For instance, Yasojima, who was ranked in the makuuchi in the late eighteenth century, was still competing in the makushita when he was nearly sixty. Tanikaze, too, remained active in the sport until his death from influenza at the age of forty-four in 1795.

Tanikaze and Onogawa were succeeded by the invincible ozeki Raiden Tameemon, possibly the strongest rikishi of all time. Because the feudal lord

This woodblock print by Shunsho shows a pre-bout ritual between the two yokozuna Tanikaze (left) and Onogawa, circa 1790. The print would have appeared soon after the bout, filling a role similar to that of today's baseball cards. Collection of the Tokyo National Museum.

50

This woodblock print by Kuniteru from about 1845 depicts a scene in the shitakubeya. Yokozuna Shiranui Dakuemon is shown on the extreme right, having his tsuna tied in preparation for the ring-entering ceremony. The rikishi standing next to him will serve as his two attendants. Collection of the Sumo Museum.

who sponsored him was not particularly powerful, Raiden was never named to the rank of yokozuna, which was then still honorary. He stayed at ozeki for sixteen years—an all-time record—although he was never defeated in successive bouts. He recorded a total of 258 wins and only ten losses during his twenty-two years in the makuuchi.

Raiden was heavy, even slightly larger than Tanikaze. Raiden kept a diary for most of his life, which covers the peak years of his sumo career. In it he notes his frequent travels to and from Edo, Kyoto, Osaka and the provinces, but only once mentions a honbasho in which he took part.

Raiden's is not the only case of a great ozeki's being denied, or forced to turn down, the honorary rank of yokozuna. Kashiwado Risuke and Tamagaki Gakunosuke, ozeki of nearly Raiden's caliber, were offered the honor as well, but were compelled to refuse due to conflicting feudal loyalties.

During the Edo period other yokozuna, including Onomatsu, Inazuma, Unryu and Jinmaku were great rikishi, whereas Shiranui Dakuemon, Hidenoyama and Shiranui Koemon were simply lucky to have influential backers.

Edo-period rikishi owed their livelihood to the *daimyo*, or feudal lords. The top rikishi were given samurai status, and thus, like warriors, were allowed to carry two swords with them.

The system of daimyo sponsorship that arose during that period resembles the modern tradition of corporate patronage. Sponsoring lords of the feudal period originated the tradition of presenting their rikishi with heavy, decorative aprons, or *keshomawashi*. At the time these were emblazoned with the daimyo's own family crest. The loyalty of the rikishi ran deep. In the final years of turmoil marking the end of the shogunate, some assisted their masters on the battlefield.

The powerful daimyo were sometimes known to dispute decisions that went against their rikishi, and even to demand that a draw be declared or a rematch held.

Kunisada's woodblock print, "A panoramic view of a sumo tournament," shows a bout held at the Eko-in temple in Edo in about 1832. The geometric patterns decorating the keshomawashi aprons represent the family crests of each man's patron among the feudal lords, or *daimyo*. Thus the two men in orange standing on the ring proper would have been sponsored by the same daimyo. Collection of the Sumo Museum.

Raiden, considered by many the strongest rikishi of all time, is the subject of this wood-block print by Shuntei. From the Draeger Collection. Courtesy of Phil Relnick.

This woodblock print shows the rikishi of the time transporting the shogunate's gift of huge bags of rice to Commodore Perry's ships in 1854. Collection of the Tsubouchi Memorial Theater Museum, Waseda University.

In 1853, the declining shogunate faced its first challenge from outside when Commodore Matthew Perry's *kurofune*, or black ships, sailed into Edo Bay, demanding that Japan conduct diplomatic negotiations with the United States. The shogunate put the Americans off as long as possible, but Perry obtained his agreement the following year. At the same time he got a demonstration of sumo.

When the American warships prepared to depart in 1854 they were well stocked with presents from the Japanese government. Most of the gifts were aboard when the Japanese officials announced that there was still one more: hundreds of 120-pound (54.5-kilogram) bags of rice lying on shore. The Japanese proudly brought out a group of about twenty-five rikishi who were enlisted to carry the rice to the pier. The authorities then invited their American guests to watch a series of matches. There is evidence to suggest that Perry and his men were the first Westerners to see sumo.

The Meiji and Taisho Periods (1868–1926)

The collapse of the Tokugawa shogunate in 1868 threatened sumo's very survival, since it put an end to the daimyo's sponsorship of individual competitors. Sumo's popularity waned as the resistance to foreign influence seen at the time of Commodore Perry's first visit gave way, just fifteen years later, to a mad rush to Westernize Japanese culture. Sumo's nationwide organization began to fracture; the Kyoto and Osaka sumo associations became independent from the Tokyo group. Previously many of the same rikishi had been listed on the banzuke used in these three cities, but by around 1870 the official ranking sheets became completely distinct.

Interest in sumo—and the association's funds—bottomed out in the 1870s.

To make matters worse, a maegashira named Takasago Uragoro rebelled in Tokyo in 1873, demanding reforms to sumo's organization and system of remuneration that would bring the sport more closely into step with the modernity of the new era. He was expelled from the Tokyo ranks and formed a small rival association.

In May 1878, a compromise settlement was reached between the Tokyo sumo organization and the Takasago group. Takasago retired from active competition and was appointed a director of the Tokyo body.

Takasago, who also acted as a *shisho*, or master of a heya, raised a number of strong rikishi, including yokozuna Nishinoumi I and Konishiki. In his final years, Takasago's dictatorial ways and alleged favoritism in assigning rankings were met with strikes by the rikishi. Still, he played an instrumental role in ensuring sumo's survival in a dramatically transformed society.

The Meiji emperor was an enthusiastic sumo fan. His attendance at exhibition matches in the 1880s greatly increased the sport's respectability. He also passed his love for sumo on to his grandson, the Showa emperor, and great-grandson, the current emperor.

The greatest yokozuna of early Meiji was Umegatani I, who reached his peak as an ozeki in the early 1880s. He would have been small for a rikishi by today's standards, but had an exceptionally strong constitution. He achieved a remarkable makuuchi record of 116 wins and just six losses. He led the precursor of the present-day Sumo Association following his retirement, and outlived all his contemporaries, including his son-in-law Umegatani II. He died in 1928 at eighty-three, and is still the only yokozuna to have succumbed to old age.

The rank of yokozuna was listed on the banzuke for the first time in May 1890, when Nishinoumi I was promoted to the rank. Takasago-beya, which housed Nishinoumi and Konishiki, and Ikazuchi-beya, which raised the former Umegatani I, were the most powerful heya at the close of the nineteenth century.

After a series of relatively unimpressive yokozuna had run their course, Hitachiyama and Umegatani II were promoted jointly to yokozuna in 1903. Umegatani II was just twenty-six, and Hitachiyama twenty-nine, which made both unusually young for the time. Hitachiyama's power approached that of Umegatani I, while the short and pot-bellied Umegatani II was surprisingly skillful, considering his tremendous weight.

Hitachiyama also had a dynamic personality that enabled him to recruit many fine rikishi away from the declining Osaka and Kyoto sumo associations. This strained the relations between Tokyo's and Osaka's sumo organizations. Relations were severed in 1910 when Tokyo refused to recognize the promotion of Osaka rikishi Okido to yokozuna. This situation continued for two years, until the promotion was finally officially acknowledged.

Hitachiyama and Umegatani II's unprecedented popularity gave the Tokyo Sumo Association the impetus it needed to build the first Kokugikan in Ryogoku in 1909.

The earliest attempts to bring sumo to world attention were made during this period. Hitachiyama travelled to the United States in 1907, where he met twice with President Theodore Roosevelt at the White House. In 1910 a delegation from the Kyoto sumo association, headed by yokozuna Oikari and

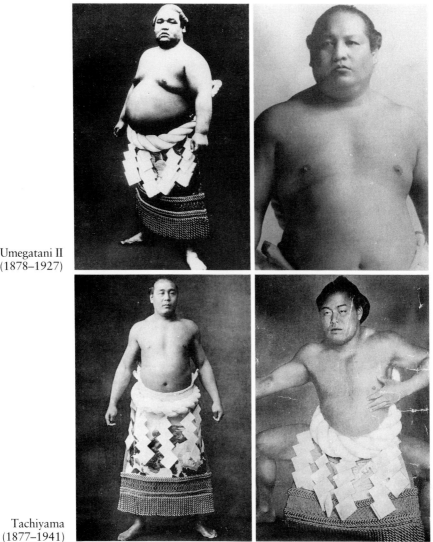

Umegatani II
(1878–1927)

Hitachiyama
(1874–1922)

Tachiyama
(1877–1941)

Tochigiyama
(1892–1959)

including several figures listed at makuuchi on the Kyoto banzuke, took part in an exposition in London marking the first full-scale presentation of professional sumo overseas. Unfortunately, the sponsors of the trip did not provide transportation back to Japan, and Oikari ended his days as a dockyard worker in Chile. Tokyo rikishi also toured Hawaii and the west coast of the United States three times during the Taisho period (1912–26).

Tachiyama was promoted to yokozuna in 1911, and soon eclipsed Hitachiyama and Umegatani. He lost only three bouts during his seven years as a yokozuna. Tachiyama was much taller and heavier than his rivals, with an imposing physique that recalled that of Edo-period greats like Tanikaze and Raiden.

Tachiyama was succeeded by Tochigiyama and Onishiki, who had both been raised by Hitachiyama. Tochigiyama was fifty kilograms lighter than Tachiyama but used equally effective aggressive thrusting tactics. Like Chiyonofuji in the late 1980s, Tochigiyama distinguished himself as a "small but great" yokozuna.

Leading rikishi staged a walkout in the Shinbashi Club Incident of 1911, seeking more money and other reforms. This conflict was quickly resolved and brought no significant changes. The Mikawashima Incident in January 1923 was more serious. When mediation by yokozuna Onishiki failed, most of the top rikishi locked themselves in a factory in Mikawashima. The police then intervened, and rikishi received an increase in the amount of their retirement benefits. Onishiki, though, severed his own mage and retired just after the conflict was settled, to take responsibility.

The Showa Period (1926–1989)

In 1925, the nearly-bankrupt Osaka sumo association merged with the group in Tokyo to form the new Dai-Nihon Sumo Kyokai (All-Japan Sumo Association; the "Dai-," or "All-," was dropped from the name in 1958). Tournaments were held in 1926 to determine the rankings for the new banzuke which would include rikishi from both Tokyo and Osaka. The Osaka rikishi took a thrashing from their Tokyo counterparts, with even Osaka yokozuna Miyagiyama inferior to the Tokyo komusubi and sekiwake.

In January 1927, just days after Emperor Showa's accession to the throne, the first official tournament was held under the amalgamated banzuke. One former Osaka ozeki had performed so poorly in 1926 that he was ranked in the makushita. Miyagiyama was retained as a yokozuna only because there was no precedent for demoting a yokozuna, and to help Osaka save face.

Miyagiyama created a sensation in January 1927 by winning the *yusho*, or championship, and in the process defeating some of Tokyo's best.

Four official tournaments were held annually from 1927 to 1932: in January and May in Tokyo at the Kokugikan, and in March and September or October in Osaka, Kyoto, Nagoya, Hiroshima or Fukuoka.

During this period, early in the reign of the Showa emperor, the turnout at sumo tournaments was quite poor. There were three yokozuna, but one, Tsunenohana, was so much stronger than the others that he had no credible rivals. The slow and ailing Nishinoumi III retired in 1928, followed two years

Miyagiyama performs the yokozuna dohyo-iri. Early Showa period.

later by Tsunenohana himself, who withdrew abruptly while still in his prime, leaving Miyagiyama as the only yokozuna.

Radio broadcasts began in 1928. Initially some members of the Sumo Association put up strong resistance, arguing that live coverage would reduce attendance at honbasho. However, Dewanoumi Oyakata (former komusubi Ryogoku and at the time the *de facto* leader of the association) sensed that radio would in fact help increase attendance at the Kokugikan, as it soon began to do.

The early and mid-1930s were a turbulent period in Japanese history, marked by assassinations, attempted military coup d'états and strikes. The sumo world was not immune to the social climate: in early January 1932, every member of the Dewanoumi ichimon from the makuuchi went on strike, demanding radical reforms including abolition of the east-west system of listing rikishi on the banzuke and an end to the oyakata system. Soon nearly everyone ranked at makuuchi had joined the strike. This rebellion, led by sekiwake Tenryu Saburo, was the most serious in sumo's history, and nearly destroyed the Sumo Association.

The two sides attempted to negotiate, but the rebels refused to compromise, resulting in an outright schism. The rebels ultimately named their group the Dai-Nihon Kansai Zumo Kyokai (All-Japan Kansai Sumo Association) and set up headquarters in Osaka. At first, the Kansai tournaments attracted a good deal of attention but, in time, fans grew bored with the elimination format used in tournaments there. As some rikishi began drifting back to Tokyo, the rival group's popularity declined. In addition, the start of Futabayama's meteoric rise in Tokyo made uncomfortably clear how few powerful rikishi were emerging in Osaka to replace the old guard.

After a final tournament in August 1937, Tenryu disbanded his association. At the end of the year, he returned the rikishi wishing to continue their careers to Dewanoumi-beya, ending a five-year rebellion that had nearly done away with some of sumo's most time-honored traditions.

Attendance at the Kokugikan soared when Futabayama rose from maegashira to yokozuna in just four tournaments and reached the sport's highest rank in May 1937. This led the Sumo Association to extend the number of days in the honbasho, first to thirteen in May 1937, and then to fifteen in May 1939.

Futabayama, unlike many overwhelmingly powerful yokozuna, was extremely popular. His good looks and elegant style combined to raise him to the status of a national hero just before and during World War II. Futabayama won sixty-nine consecutive bouts between January 1936 and January 1939.

Sumo and World War II

The public's enthusiasm for sumo was undiminished throughout the war. The government discouraged sports with American origins, such as pro baseball, promoting instead the traditional martial arts—judo, aikido, kendo and, of course, sumo. Futabayama maintained dominance of the sport until May 1943, when he won his twelfth and final championship.

By 1943, Japan had clearly lost the advantage in the war and, throughout the country, living conditions declined sharply. The effects of rationing were

Futabayama, the dignified and handsome yokozuna who became a national hero just before and during World War II

dramatic, with many rikishi losing as much as one-third of their weight. Some, particularly those ranked in the lower divisions, were drafted into the army or navy, while many higher-ranking rikishi left on the home front were organized into labor brigades and sent to work in factories during the last years of the war. Honbasho were still held at the Kokugikan until January 1944, when the Japanese army appropriated the building for use as a balloon bomb factory. The May and November tournaments that year were held at a temporary, open-air dohyo erected at the Korakuen baseball stadium. These drew seventy thousand people, the largest crowds ever assembled to watch sumo.

The incendiary bombs dropped in the Great Tokyo Air Raid of March 10–11, 1945, almost completely destroyed the Ryogoku area. Fire gutted the Kokugikan, rendering it useless to the army. Most of the heya soon moved out to the suburbs, or to neighboring cities, to escape the continuing bombing.

Two makuuchi rikishi, Toyoshima and Matsuuragata, were killed in the fires of the March 10–11 air raid. However, nearly all the other rikishi, including those sent to the front lines, survived the war.

The last wartime tournament was held in the severely-damaged Kokugi-kan in June 1945. The Sumo Association, concerned about the possibility of further bombing, sold no tickets. The only people in attendance were those connected with sumo and a number of war-wounded. Competition was held with no lighting, a shattered roof and a simple dohyo marked out on the ground. The great Futabayama dropped out after the first day, and was never to compete again.

Postwar Chaos

Rikishi were scattered throughout Japan when the Japanese government announced its acceptance of the Potsdam Declaration on August 15, 1945. Most who had not been drafted were working in war-related industries, and only occasionally participating in exhibition matches.

After Japan's surrender, the Sumo Association's main concern was to ascertain the occupying forces' stance toward sumo, and find out whether the sport would be allowed to survive intact. Initial contact with the Americans was made in September 1945, apparently by Musashigawa Oyakata (the former maegashira Dewanohana) and by Kasagiyama, who was then still an active rikishi and who could speak some English. The Americans soon gave the go-ahead for a honbasho to be held at the Ryogoku Kokugikan in November 1945.

The Sumo Association immediately enlarged the dohyo, hoping to make the sport more pleasing to the occupying authorities. This move drew vehement protests from many rikishi and oyakata. The association pressed ahead, and managed to borrow money to repair the Kokugikan's shattered roof and charred interior.

In spite of these difficulties and the desperate poverty of most of Tokyo's residents, the Aki Basho of November 1945 was very successful. The ten-day tournament brought in a full house each day, and generated total proceeds sufficient to keep the Sumo Association operating. Futabayama did not compete at all; he announced his retirement toward the end of the basho, citing the enlarged dohyo as his reason. In fact, he is said to have decided to retire in November 1944 after losing to the young maegashira Azumafuji, who would later become a yokozuna.

With Futabayama gone and yokozuna Akinoumi and Terukuni in poor shape, a fourth yokozuna, Haguroyama, finally came into his own, winning the yusho with a perfect 10-0 record. New maegashira Chiyonoyama drew some of the attention to himself during the same tournament when he also won every bout he fought.

The Supreme Command of the Allied Powers expropriated the Kokugikan in December 1945 for use as a skating rink and auditorium. The Sumo Association was not able to obtain permission to use the building at all during the first half of 1946. A shortage of food in the cities compelled management to spend much of 1946 arranging exhibition bouts in the countryside. These matches were staged mainly to give the rikishi and other sumo personnel enough to eat. While the Japanese transportation and distribution systems were in a shambles, the countryside was relatively affluent. Farmers supplied rice and other staples in exchange for entry to these performances.

The rikishi returned to Tokyo for a thirteen-day honbasho held at the former Kokugikan in November 1946. After the tournament the Allies granted free use of the stadium for Futabayama's retirement ceremony, the last sumo event to be held in the old Kokugikan.

The Sumo Kyokai was no longer able to hold honbasho in the former sumo arena after 1946, but obtained permission to stage basho at the Meiji Jingu Gaien, or the outer gardens of Meiji Shrine, beginning in June 1947. A ramshackle arena was constructed, but since it had no roof, tournaments once again had to be suspended in inclement weather, just as they had in the eighteenth and nineteenth centuries.

An old rival of Haguroyama's, Maedayama, became the first yokozuna of the postwar period in June 1947, after spending nearly a decade as ozeki in the shadow of the overwhelming Futabayama. But Azumafuji and another young rikishi, Chiyonoyama, soon took over the spotlight from the survivors of the Futabayama era. Haguroyama returned to action in 1949, after having been sidelined by an injury for more than a year, but no longer had any advantage over the younger yokozuna and ozeki.

The aging Haguroyama survived in active competition until September 1953, and took the yusho in January 1952 with a perfect 15-0 record, a remarkable achievement for a thirty-seven-year-old. He held the yokozuna rank for a total of twelve years and three months, an all-time record.

Television was introduced to Japan in 1953. The *shihon-bashira*, or four pillars that had traditionally supported the dohyo's roof, were removed in

Yoshibayama, a yokozuna who had the potential to be great but whose career was interrupted by several years of active duty in the Second World War

Tochinishiki (photo courtesy of Sankei Sports)

1952. The yakata was suspended instead from the building's ceiling, which facilitated the start of sumo television broadcasts the following year.

Kagamisato was promoted to yokozuna in January 1953, as was Yoshibayama in January 1954. Both were among the heaviest rikishi of their generation, and might well have became outstanding yokozuna had they not lost several of their formative years to military service.

New Heroes of the TV Era

The early years at the Kuramae Kokugikan coincided with the rise of the two great yokozuna of the 1950s, Tochinishiki and Wakanohana I. Both were unlikely candidates for yokozuna, weighing under 220 pounds (one hundred kilograms) when promoted to ozeki. But both were superb technicians, with exceptionally good balance and timing.

Tokitsukaze (the former Futabayama) held the office of sumo president from 1957 through his death in December 1968. During that time he carried out significant reforms, which included granting monthly salaries to rikishi

ranked at juryo and above, and instituting a mandatory retirement age for elders and referees, of sixty-five.

Tochinishiki was promoted to yokozuna in October 1954, with Wakanohana I following in January 1958. Tochinishiki had a solid, if not overly impressive, record in his first years at yokozuna. But it was only after his rival Wakanohana was also promoted that he began to show his true potential.

Tochinishiki and Wakanohana I competed together at sumo's highest rank from March 1958–May 1960, a period that became known as the Tochi-Waka era. Their presence made sumo nearly as popular as it had been in the Futabayama era.

Tochinishiki retired abruptly in May 1960. Wakanohana won two more tournaments, then gradually submitted to advancing age and the emergence of a new generation of fine rikishi ten or more years his junior.

A dramatic transfer of power occurred in 1960 with the rise of Taiho and Kashiwado. Taiho, who entered the makuuchi in January 1960 at the age of nineteen, won his first championship in November, becoming the youngest man, at that point, ever to have been promoted to ozeki. Kashiwado, two years Taiho's senior, had also earned the rank earlier that year.

The generational change was completed in the years 1960 through 1963. Taiho and Kashiwado both received promotion to yokozuna while Tochinoumi, Sadanoyama and collegian Yutakayama advanced to ozeki. The years from 1961–69 were referred to as the Hakuho era ("Haku" is an alternative reading of the character for "Kashi," and the "ho" is from "Taiho"). The last stalwarts of the Tochi-Waka years, many of whom had started their careers in the late 1930s and 1940s, were quickly swept aside.

The rivalry between the yokozuna was close at first, but Taiho soon shot far ahead of Kashiwado. Taiho went on to become nearly unbeatable. Kashiwado, on the other hand, suffered a number of injuries and won a total of only five yusho, as compared to Taiho's record thirty-two.

Sumo's popularity ebbed when Taiho began to dominate the tournament race in the mid-sixties. The Sumo Kyokai, under Tokitsukaze's leadership, attempted to remedy this slump by mandating bouts between rikishi from the same ichimon, or group of heya, from January 1965.

Younger rikishi of the Hakuho generation began to enter the sanyaku in

Taiho

1964 and 1965. However, their progress was limited by Taiho's overwhelming presence.

Yokozuna Tochinoumi retired in 1966, as did Sadanoyama in 1968. Kashiwado recovered from a long string of injuries, only to have his considerable strength sapped by diabetes. Meanwhile, Taiho challenged Futabayama's long-standing record sixty-nine-bout winning streak in late 1968 and early 1969. He had won forty-five consecutive bouts when he was upset by maegashira Toda in March 1969, in a match which slow-motion replays prove that Taiho actually won.

Tokitsukaze's successor as rijicho was Musashigawa Oyakata, the former maegashira Dewanohana. Though his career as an active rikishi in the 1930s had been undistinguished, in his five years as Sumo Association president from 1968–74, Musashigawa greatly helped popularize the sport abroad. It was during his tenure, for instance, that Hawaiian-born Takamiyama became the first foreign rikishi to win the makuuchi championship.

In July 1969, Kashiwado retired, marking the end of the Hakuho era. Tamanoumi and Kitanofuji were jointly promoted to yokozuna in January 1970, ushering in the new Kita-Tama era. Taiho won two more yusho and retired in May 1971 after losing to Takanohana, younger brother of yokozuna Wakanohana I.

Tamanoumi had the potential to be an outstanding yokozuna, but died suddenly after a long-delayed appendectomy in October 1971. In his ten tournaments as a yokozuna he had won 130 bouts and lost only twenty.

In the early seventies a new era began, centered on Wajima, Kitanoumi

Kitanoumi

Chiyonofuji, a great yokozuna of recent times

and Takanohana. Wajima, who had launched his professional career only after graduating from university in 1970, was to win a total of fourteen championships, while Kitanoumi won twenty-four and even bettered some of Taiho's records.

The entire last half of the 1970s, known as the Rinko era, was dominated by Wajima and Kitanoumi.

During the same period, Takanohana—perhaps even more popular than his elder brother had been—won two championships and was ranked at ozeki for fifty tournaments, the latter a record that will be difficult to break. Though skillful and tenacious, he was handicapped by his inability to put on weight.

Muscular, lanky Chiyonofuji was promoted to yokozuna in 1981. Meanwhile three other yokozuna—Mienoumi, Wajima and Wakanohana II—retired. The once powerful Kitanoumi went into a steady decline and retired in January 1985, after achieving his objective of competing in the new and ultramodern Kokugikan that had been completed the year before.

Chiyonofuji reached his prime only after he turned thirty in 1985. Though a relative lightweight at about 264 pounds (120 kilograms), he possessed extraordinary strength, speed and skill. Despite his advancing age, Chiyo achieved fifty-three consecutive wins in 1988, losing to fellow yokozuna Onokuni on the final day of the November 1988 tournament, in what was to be the last bout fought during the Showa period.

Akebono, sumo's first foreign-born yokozuna

The Present Day

Chiyonofuji's dominance of the sport continued into the reign of the current emperor (which started in 1989). He won thirty-one yusho—just one shy of Taiho's record, but against less impressive opposition. He was approaching his thirty-sixth birthday when he was upset by eighteen-year-old maegashira Takahanada (now Takanohana) in May 1991. Two days later, after losing another bout to komusubi Takatoriki, Chiyonofuji retired.

Soon afterward, Onokuni, Asahifuji and Hokutoumi retired as well, though all were five to eight years younger than Chiyonofuji. Hawaiian-born Konishiki came close to being named the first foreign-born yokozuna, only to be outshone by the younger, more agile Akebono. The yokozuna rank stood vacant for the first time in over sixty years in July 1992. In January 1993, while Takanohana moved up to ozeki, Akebono became the first foreigner to reach yokozuna.

Sumo's popularity rose in 1992–93 to its highest level since the Futabayama era, largely due to the presence of Takanohana and his elder brother Wakanohana. The first pair of brothers ever to be ranked at ozeki at the same time, they are also the sons of Takanohana I. With sole yokozuna Akebono receiving solid competition from Takanohana and a number of others, the current sumo boom seems likely to continue.

III

NEW LEGENDS

Sumo's Hawaiian Legacy

Hawaii is in every sense a melting pot, a hodgepodge of cultures with origins as diverse as Portugal, Polynesia, the Philippines and Japan. Hawaii was the destination of the first large-scale wave of Japanese emigration in the 1880s, following the Meiji Restoration. In contrast to the generally high level of achievement and income of today's Japanese-Americans, the first Japanese to settle in Hawaii in the late nineteenth century were extremely poor and had little choice but to work as indentured laborers in the sugar and pineapple fields.

Many Japanese maintained their interest in sumo after settling in Hawaii. In those days—long before the advent of radio or television—the *issei* (first-generation immigrants) created their own amateur sumo network extending throughout the islands, complete with regular tournaments.

As the average income of the issei wrestlers gradually rose after the turn of the century, they began to order high quality mawashi, keshomawashi and other sumo attire from Japan. Soon afterward, interest began to spread to other islanders of Japanese ancestry.

In 1913, the Tokyo Sumo Association sent nearly the entire makuuchi to

During his active career, Hawaiian-born rikishi Takamiyama became the first non-Japanese to advance to the makuuchi. He now acts as master of Azumazeki-beya, which houses Akebono. Photo by Clyde Newton.

70

perform an exhibition tournament on Oahu. Two more such occasions followed during the Taisho period (1912–1926).

Sumo's popularity quickly spread beyond first- and second-generation Japanese-Americans to people of other ethnic backgrounds on all the islands. World War II temporarily halted the sumo boom in Hawaii, but the sport's popularity picked up again soon after the war.

In the late fifties, Jesse Kuhaulua, a youth from the island of Maui who was largely of native Hawaiian ancestry, took up amateur sumo on the recommendation of his high-school football coach. He had weak legs, and thus poor balance, as the result of a traffic accident as a small boy; his coach felt that sumo would strengthen the lower half of his body.

Jesse, who as a high school junior already weighed over 220 pounds (one hundred kilograms), excelled at sumo and entered a tournament on the main island of Oahu. There he came to the attention of a sumo scout acquainted with Takasago Oyakata, the former yokozuna Maedayama.

Jesse graduated from high school and began thinking about a career as a police officer. However, in February 1964, the top-division rikishi held their second postwar exhibition tournament in Hawaii, and Jesse was there to watch. He was introduced to Takasago Oyakata, who invited him to come to Tokyo.

Takasago made history by offering Jesse Kuhaulua a place in his heya. The only non-Japanese citizens who had competed in professional sumo to that point were either of Japanese ancestry, or Koreans with at least some knowledge of Japanese.

After overcoming the opposition of his mother and other relatives, Jesse flew to Tokyo and entered Takasago-beya. The nineteen-year-old had no knowledge of the Japanese language and little of the culture, and was totally unaccustomed to Tokyo's relatively cold winters. The fact that he not only survived but prevailed, becoming close to a living legend, is a tribute to his remarkable perseverance.

Jesse was given one of Takasago-beya's time-honored *shikona*, or ring names, Takamiyama Daigoro. He made extraordinary progress, reaching the makushita level as early as November 1964, just nine months after he arrived in Japan. After a brief series of disappointing tournaments in the makushita, he regained the weight he had lost during the first months of his career, when he had had difficulty in adapting to the Japanese diet. In March 1967, he was promoted to the juryo and thus became the first rikishi of non-oriental ancestry to become a sekitori, a salaried rikishi.

Takamiyama advanced to the makuuchi in January 1968, where he was to remain until close to the end of his career. He recorded a sensational upset over yokozuna Sadanoyama in March 1968, in just the second tournament after his promotion. Despite his problems with balance, general consensus in the late sixties and early seventies held that Takamiyama might well go as far as ozeki.

Though he never made it there, he did become the first non-Japanese to win the makuuchi championship in July 1972, with a 13–2 record.

With Jesse's tournament win, and as heya took in other non-Japanese members, interest in sumo grew overseas. Within twenty years of Takamiyama's championship, official exhibitions were held in China, Europe, Latin America and other areas around the world.

Throughout his career, Jesse was extremely popular. Regardless of whether he won or lost, his bouts were always interesting. He fought to the bitter end and concluded his career as a battered thirty-nine-year-old in May 1984. His departure coincided with the rise of the second strong Hawaiian rikishi, Konishiki Yasokichi.

Konishiki set out to do what had been just beyond Jesse's reach: advance to the ranks of ozeki and yokozuna. He created a sensation in September 1984 by nearly walking off with the yusho in his second tournament in the makuuchi. He upset yokozuna Chiyonofuji and Takanosato with almost ridiculous ease. Some more conservative fans were alarmed by the unexpected appearance of this twenty-year-old upstart; a few even went so far as to compare his rise to a second coming of the black ships of Commodore Perry that had forced Japan open to the rest of the world back in the mid-nineteenth century.

At the height of his career Konishiki may have lacked technical finesse, but he had prodigious strength, and far better balance than Takamiyama. Many anticipated that he would rise rapidly to ozeki and then yokozuna, eventually becoming the sport's dominant force.

But this was not to be. While at the rank of sekiwake in 1985, Konishiki injured his right knee, which precipitated his fall back to the maegashira ranks. He quickly recovered, but had lost some of the speed and superior balance that had made him so dangerous in September 1984.

Konishiki, the first non-Japanese ever promoted to sumo's second-highest rank, of ozeki

Konishiki finally gained promotion to ozeki after the May 1987 tournament, which made him the first foreign-born rikishi to advance beyond seki-wake.

In 1988–89, Konishiki suffered a series of knee injuries that resulted in poor performances. For a time, it appeared that he might never win a championship. In November 1989, however, he made a dramatic comeback, and took the yusho at the Kyushu Basho with a fine 14–1 record.

Even after his knees and balance had recovered, Konishiki was still thwarted in his attempts to become the first foreign yokozuna. He succumbed to psychological pressure whenever he came within a few wins of promotion to yokozuna. Further, as his weight continued to increase—at one point to 264 kilograms—he had greater difficulty with agile technicians like Akinoshima.

Konishiki won his second yusho in November 1990, and his third in March 1992. In May 1990 he had almost achieved *zensho yusho*, or a perfect record, going into the final day at 14–0. But he lost that day to yokozuna Asahifuji in the final bout, and then again in a playoff. In March 1992, Konishiki had stood on the brink of promotion to yokozuna. He had achieved a 13–2 record in November 1991, a 12–3 in January 1992, and 13–2 again in March 1992. But he slipped to third place in January 1992, which disqualified him from consideration.

Konishiki overpowers Waka-nohana with a *nodowa*, or thrust to the throat.

Konishiki would probably have been promoted with a 13–2 or 14–1 record in May 1992, and either the yusho or runner-up honors. But this was the turning point of his career, and he has never since figured in a race for a yusho.

In November 1993, Konishiki failed to achieve *kachikoshi* (a winning record) in his second consecutive tournament, and thus lost the ozeki ranking he had held over the course of thirty-six basho and for more than six years.

Now, at age thirty, Konishiki has dropped to the maegashira ranks and is a shadow of the formidable ozeki he once was. He has acquired Japanese citizenship and plans to stay in sumo as an oyakata with Takasago-beya, rather than branching out on his own, as Takamiyama did when he formed the Azumazeki-beya upon his retirement from the ring.

Although he has never managed to achieve his ambition of becoming a yokozuna, Konishiki is destined to go down in history as a great ozeki.

His bout against Akebono in May 1991 was the first between two non-oriental rikishi ranked in the makuuchi. Akebono won their first meeting, after which point Konishiki took the upper hand and held it until the spring of 1992.

In January 1993 Akebono became the first non-Japanese to be promoted to yokozuna. He then set about winning four tournaments that year. For the first time in sumo history, a non-Japanese clearly dominated the sport. A fourth Hawaiian, Musashimaru, was promoted to ozeki in January 1994, as Konishiki's decline sent him back down the ranks to maegashira.

The four Hawaiian rikishi—the now-retired Takamiyama, and after him Konishiki, Akebono and Musashimaru—have been instrumental in generating interest in sumo around the world. The sport remains Japanese, but is now beginning to gain the international appreciation it so richly deserves.

Musashimaru shows his strength and determination.

Akebono wins the bout shown on the preceding page, with *uwatenage* (an overarm throw).

Akebono

Akebono is the sixty-fourth yokozuna in sumo's history, and the first foreign-born rikishi to reach sumo's highest rank. He was born on the Hawaiian island of Oahu in May 1969, as Chad George Haheo Rowan. Chad is the eldest of Randy and Janis Rowan's four children. Randy, who died in 1993, was of Irish, native Hawaiian and Chinese ancestry, while Chad's mother Janis is of native Hawaiian and Cuban heritage.

Already very tall as a teenager, Chad was one of the star players on his high school basketball team. During his senior year of high school in 1987, he was spotted—at his grandfather's funeral—by Larry Aweou, a relative of Azumazeki Oyakata (the former sekiwake Takamiyama). At first, Aweou and Azumazeki Oyakata were interested in Chad's younger brother, who was a little shorter. But since the younger boy still had a year of high school left to finish, Azumazeki Oyakata took Chad in his place.

When Chad entered sumo in March 1988, together with the future Takanohana, Wakanohana and other promising rikishi, he was over two meters tall. Azumazeki believed that, given his height, Chad would be lucky to go beyond the juryo or lower maegashira levels at best. Chad's first shikona was Taikai, which was changed to Akebono when he advanced to jonokuchi in May 1988.

Akebono undertook a rigorous training program and made surprisingly fast progress for so tall a rikishi. He was promoted to the juryo in March 1990, just two years after his debut. He had a number of close, exciting bouts with the Waka-Taka brothers, beginning in 1988, which showed that he had as much promise as did the sons of the former ozeki Takanohana I.

Akebono breezed through the juryo in three tournaments, and was promoted to the makuuchi in September 1990, just behind Takahanada and together with Wakahanada. He was promoted to komusubi in March 1991 and to sekiwake for the following tournament, where, however, he suffered the first losing record of his career, a close 7 wins and 8 losses.

In January 1992, Akebono achieved a fine 13-2 record as a komusubi, while Takahanada won his first yusho. Akebono's disappointment at not win-

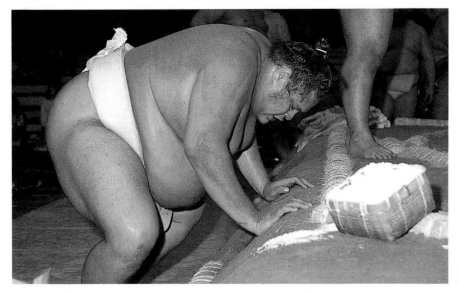

Akebono finishes practice during a regional exhibition.

ning that tournament seems to have provided the incentive he needed, because he won the May 1992 tournament, as a sekiwake, with a 13-2 record, thereby gaining promotion to ozeki before any of his peers.

An injury forced Akebono to sit out the first tournament held after he advanced to sumo's second-highest rank, but he immediately came back to win consecutive yusho in November 1992 and January 1993, with which he advanced to yokozuna.

At over 480 pounds, or 220 kilograms, Akebono has the brute strength that Takanohana and Wakanohana lack. Though his balance is superior to that of his Hawaiian seniors Takamiyama and Konishiki, he is at his best when using thrusting or pushing tactics. He is virtually unbeatable when his opponents fail to get a grip on his mawashi.

Akebono won three consecutive championships, from July through November 1993, but has yet to achieve a perfect 15-0 record. Nevertheless, he has set on his sights on becoming a great yokozuna. With seven yusho to his credit by March 1994 and still only twenty-four years of age, he may win a career total of twenty or more championships.

Akebono has made a great effort to master Japanese, and has stated that he hopes someday to follow in the footsteps of Takamiyama and Konishiki by applying for Japanese citizenship and staying on in sumo as an oyakata after retirement.

Wakanohana and Takanohana

Takanohana

Waka and Taka are the first brothers to hold the rank of ozeki at the same time. They are the sons of former ozeki Takanohana I and nephews of former yokozuna Wakanohana I. The young brothers' phenomenal popularity was largely responsible for the sumo boom that started in the early 1990s.

Takanohana I, now Futagoyama Oyakata and head of the heya that includes his two sons, married early. Surprisingly, he is slightly closer in age to his eldest son Wakanohana than to his own brother, former yokozuna Wakanohana I, who is twenty-two years his senior.

Wakanohana was born as Hanada Masaru in January 1971. His younger brother Takanohana, whose real name is Hanada Koji, followed in August 1972. Having been immersed in the world of sumo from

Wakanohana (left) and younger brother Takanohana

childhood, the two boys had decided to seek a career in the sport even before their father retired from active competition in 1981. Koji appears to have had the stronger interest; as soon as he completed junior high school in February 1988, he begged his reluctant father to take him into his heya (then Fujishima-beya). Masaru, then in his second year of high school, decided to drop out and start his sumo career at the same time.

The two boys made their debut in March 1988, Masaru competing as Wakahanada, and Koji as Takahanada. Wakahanada took the lead at first by winning the jonokuchi championship in May 1988, but Takahanada soon began to outperform his older brother. Though Takahanada's weight dropped more than twenty-two pounds (ten kilograms) after he entered sumo, he developed a muscular frame through relentless training.

In May 1989, Takahanada, still only sixteen, became the youngest rikishi in history to win the makushita championship. He became the youngest juryo rikishi on record in November the same year, and set yet another record for youth when he reached the makuuchi in May 1990. Wakahanada followed close behind, reaching the juryo in March 1990.

Takahanada achieved a sensational upset by defeating the aging yokozuna Chiyonofuji on the first day of the May 1991 tournament. A seventeen-year age difference separated Takahanada and the yokozuna, with Takahanada just eighteen at the time, and Chiyonofuji nearing thirty-six. Never before had so young a rikishi competed at that high a level, let alone upset a yokozuna.

Chiyonofuji retired two days later. The veteran yokozuna had vied with Takanohana's father a number of times, and an upset in November 1980 had been a key factor in the elder Takanohana's retirement during the following tournament. Chiyonofuji joked that perhaps history would repeat itself if his five-year-old son sought a sumo career in the future and upset an aging Takahanada.

Chiyonofuji's departure marked the end of one era, but Takahanada, Wakahanada, Akebono and the other promising young rikishi were not quite ready to fill his shoes. Takahanada set additional records for age at promotion to komusubi in July 1991, and to sekiwake in September that same year. After dropping temporarily to a maegashira rank in January 1992, he won the makuuchi yusho at nineteen and was presented with the Emperor's Cup, or Tenno-shihai, by his uncle, Futagoyama Oyakata, in one of the latter's last appearances as president of the Sumo Kyokai.

Takahanada became the youngest ozeki on record in January 1993, and in honor of this promotion his ring name (*shikona*) was changed to Takanohana, after his illustrious father. However, he just missed becoming the youngest yokozuna, falling short of promotion in 1993, the requisite year, by one or two wins. In January 1994 he won his fourth championship and seemed to be nearing the elusive goal.

Elder brother Wakahanada began to show his true potential only in 1993, when he won the March yusho as a komusubi and then gained promotion to ozeki after the July tournament. With this step up he took the shikona of his uncle, Wakanohana.

Takanohana now weighs more than 308 pounds (140 kilograms) and concentrates on straightforward *yotsuzumo*, or reliance primarily on grips on the opponent's mawashi. Wakanohana is shorter and somewhat underweight at 264 pounds (120 kilograms), but a very skillful technician. Wakanohana is unlikely to become his younger brother's equal, but may, like Takanohana, have the potential to become a yokozuna.

Until 1993, the handsome Takanohana was the more popular of the two. With Wakanohana's dramatic rise from maegashira to ozeki over the course of January–July 1993, fans' interest shifted for a time to the elder brother. As of 1994, with Takanohana nearing yokozuna and Wakanohana turning in solid performances at the ozeki level, the two are about equally popular.

Below, left: Takanohana launches into the tachi-ai against Kotonishiki. Right: Wakanohana against Konishiki.

New Ozeki Takanonami and Musashimaru

Takanonami and Musashimaru are the first two sekiwake to be promoted jointly to ozeki since January 1977. Both were born in 1971, which makes them the youngest pair of new ozeki in the twentieth century. Though neither has yet won a yusho, their 12-3 and 13-2 records in the two basho preceding their promotion indicate that they have the potential to do so in the near future.

Taka and Musashi have radically different styles in the ring. Takanonami is a purely defensive rikishi, with a notoriously poor tachi-ai. However, his defense is remarkably good, especially considering that his height of six foot four inches (1.95 meters) gives him a relatively high center of gravity. Musashimaru, on the other hand, is at his best when he demonstrates a strong tachi-ai and a relentless follow-up attack, as he did in the two basho prior to his promotion. Though Musashimaru is able to hold his own at yotsuzumo (grips on the opponent's belt), he is almost invariably unable to bring his awesome strength to bear when forced onto the defensive.

They also have very different personalities: whereas Takanonami is cheerful and talkative, Musashimaru is a man of few words.

What the two rikishi have in common is powerful rivals within their own heya. Takanonami is one of ten sekitori from the Futagoyama-beya and the heya's third ozeki. Thus he faces only two of the rikishi ranked above sekiwake—Akebono and Musashimaru. Takanonami made his debut in March 1987, a year before Wakanohana and Takanohana, but until recently had been overshadowed by the popular brothers. Musashimaru also will almost certainly have a stablemate at his level in the not-too-distant future; Musoyama moved up to sekiwake in March 1994 and has the potential to reach ozeki in the near future.

Takanonami was born near the Misawa U.S. Air Force base in Aomori Prefecture on October 27, 1971, the second son of a civil servant. His real name is Namioka Sadahiro. He took up sumo while in the fourth grade of elementary school, when he was already the tallest boy in his class. The junior high school he attended had closed its sumo club earlier, for lack of interest, but reopened it soon after Sadahiro enrolled, because of the great promise he showed.

Sadahiro had initially intended to continue on to high school. But by the time of his graduation from junior high, he had grown to six foot four (1.92 meters), and word of a remarkably tall boy living in Misawa had begun to circulate among Tokyo's heya. Tatsutagawa Oyakata (former sekiwake Aonosato) and Magaki Oyakata (former yokozuna Wakanohana II) first made efforts to recruit him. Azumazeki Oyakata (former sekiwake Takamiyama) also tried hard to bring the boy into his heya. However, personal connections gained Sadahiro and his parents—all fans of Takanohana I—an introduction to the retired ozeki himself, who was then oyakata of Fujishima-beya.

Sadahiro made his debut with this heya in March 1987, under his surname, Namioka. He began to achieve notice early, while ranked in the sandanme and makushita levels. In March 1991, when he was only nineteen, he was promoted to juryo. He entered the makuuchi in November 1991.

Musashimaru   Takanonami

At first, Takanonami made little progress beyond the mid-maegashira ranks, because of a weak tachi-ai. However, he sharpened his defense—nearly perfecting it, in fact—after reaching komusubi in May 1993. He had a surprisingly strong 10–5 record as a new komusubi, which he followed up with 9–6, 10–5, 12–3 and 13–2 records at sekiwake. In January 1994, he narrowly upset Akebono for the first time, finishing with runner-up honors and recording his career best of 13–2.

Musashimaru—whose real name is Fuamalu Penitani—was born in American Samoa on May 2, 1971, and moved to Hawaii with his parents and seven brothers and sisters at the age of ten. He spoke both Samoan and English fluently by the time he graduated from high school in 1989 and was brought to Japan by Musashigawa Oyakata. He is now working on making Japanese his third language.

Musashigawa Oyakata had previously taken another promising youth from Hawaii into his heya, giving him the ring name Musashibo. Musashibo was thought to have even more potential than Konishiki, but homesickness led him to leave Japan when he was still in the jonidan. Musashigawa had some misgivings about taking in another foreigner, and at first only accepted Fuamalu on a three-month trial basis. But Musashimaru soon made a good impression, training hard, working with weights, eating everything given to him and making an effort to communicate with his seniors in the Musashigawa-beya.

Fuamalu was thus formally accepted as a *deshi*, or heya member, and made his debut in September 1989. During his four-and-a-half year career, he has only once turned in a losing record, when he was in the makushita. He reached juryo in July 1991, and makuuchi in November of the same year, together with Takanonami. He went on to komusubi in May 1992, and seki-wake that September. He was close to promotion to ozeki that November, with a 9–2 record going into the twelfth day, following on 11–4 and 10–5 marks. However, he lost all four remaining bouts, and finished at 9–6.

Musashimaru won ten bouts at sekiwake in January and March 1993, but gradually declined over the next few basho. In September he came close to losing the rank, when he stood at 5–7 after the twelfth day. He barely eked out an 8–7 record in that tournament, but then snapped out of his slump and finally showed his true potential when he defeated Akebono in November and went on to a playoff against the yokozuna. He defeated Akebono again in January, and would have faced Takanohana and Takanonami in a play-off had he not stepped out a split second too soon on the final day.

Takanonami and Musashimaru have both become more self-confident in recent tournaments. The challenge facing Takanonami will be to develop a strong tachi-ai and a better offensive. If he succeeds, he will likely become a serious candidate for yokozuna. Musashimaru, on the other hand, needs to concentrate on further developing his already powerful tsukioshi tactics and relying on belt grips only as a last resort. He has the potential to reach sumo's highest rank if he can maintain his current stability over the long term.

Takanonami uses the technique *uwatenage* successfully against Kotofuji.

New Hopes

Musoyama, like Musashimaru a member of Musashigawa-beya, is expected to become a yokozuna. Born in 1972, he dropped out of university at the beginning of 1993 and was allowed to enter sumo at *makushita tsukedashi*, the rank at the bottom of the makushita where special provision is made for qualified former collegiate champions to begin their professional careers. Musoyama, whose nickname is "Kaibutsu," or "Monster," won two consecutive makushita championships in January and March 1993, and was promoted to the juryo that May. He achieved promotion to the makuuchi in September 1993, and was boosted to sekiwake in March 1994.

Musoyama has tremendous potential, as he demonstrated in his upset of yokozuna Akebono in January 1994, just one year after beginning his sumo career. Musoyama often unleashes a fierce, destructive barrage of thrusts on opponents at the beginning of bouts. If they survive this, he sometimes switches over to yotsuzumo, another technique at which he excels.

Kotonishiki has been a perennial candidate for ozeki over the last few years. Born in 1968, he entered Sadogatake-beya in 1984 and reached the makuuchi in 1989. He won the makuuchi yusho in September 1991 and has been close to ozeki several times. Though quite short at five foot eight (1.76 meters), he is a powerful thruster and—when in good condition—has one of the best tachi-ai in sumo today.

Though still a candidate for ozeki, Kotonishiki tends to be erratic. His sumo is only effective when he stays on the move, and when he begins with a poor tachi-ai he is easily defeated. Though strong enough to have seldom recorded a *makekoshi*, or losing record, Kotonishiki has nevertheless had difficulty achieving consecutive double-digit winning records.

Takatoriki of Futagoyama-beya is a contemporary of Kotonishiki's and, like him, has gone as far as sekiwake. Born in 1967, Takatoriki entered sumo in 1983. He was at his best in 1991 when he held a *sanyaku* rank over the course of several consecutive tournaments. In May that year he upset the great yokozuna Chiyonofuji, in what was to be the veteran's final bout. Like Kotonishiki, Takatoriki is of less than average height, and must keep moving to avoid losing. When at his best he is a dangerous opponent for any sanyaku rikishi. At twenty-six, Takatoriki is unlikely to become an ozeki but probably still has several good years left in his career. He is married to the youngest daughter of former yokozuna Taiho.

Akinoshima, also from Futagoyama-beya, was a strong ozeki candidate until 1992. He boasts outstanding technique and superb balance, and is about the same size as Kotonishiki and Takatoriki. Born in 1967, he entered sumo in 1982. He and Kotonishiki were the first rikishi of their generation to reach the juryo and makuuchi levels.

Akinoshima was for several years one of the most dangerous opponents for ozeki and yokozuna. His low center of gravity helped make him ozeki Konishiki's nemesis for several years. Though he has never won more than eleven bouts in the makuuchi, he was the strongest candidate for promotion to ozeki in 1990–91, until he was outperformed by the Hanada brothers. At twenty-six, Akinoshima is still young, but has been in a protracted slump recently as a result of injuries. To date, however, while ranked as a maegashira,

Musoyama during the *makuuchi dohyo-iri*

Kotonishiki entering the ring

Takatoriki during the pre-bout rituals

Akinoshima is known as an upsetter of higher-ranking rikishi. Here he is shown beating Konishiki with *uwatedashinage*.

Mainoumi, the smallest man in the makunouchi

Kyokudozan

Tomonohana, the former high school teacher nicknamed "Sensei"

he has achieved a career record fifteen *kinboshi*, or yokozuna upsets.

College graduates Mainoumi and Tomonohana are among the most colorful figures in the makuuchi today. Mainoumi is the shortest of all salaried rikishi, and at 209 pounds (ninety-five kilograms) the lightest man in the makuuchi, but his unorthodox tachi-ai and ability to tackle much larger opponents from a submarine-like position have made him dangerous. Now twenty-six, he has yet to go beyond the mid-maegashira ranks. His objective is to reach sanyaku at least once.

Tomonohana, a former high school phys-ed instructor whose nickname is "Sensei," or "Teacher," became the oldest new recruit in over sixty years at his debut in March 1992. Nearly twenty-eight at the time, and not much bigger than Mainoumi, Tomonohana was thought to have little chance of advancing beyond the juryo. He confounded the skeptics, reaching the makuuchi in 1993 and komusubi in January 1994. His 4–11 record at komusubi was the first makekoshi of his career. Tomonohana, a member of Tatsunami-beya, is now nearing his thirtieth birthday, but probably still has the best years of his career ahead of him. He may yet go as far as sekiwake.

Skillful Kyokudozan of Oshima-beya, who has gone as far as komusubi, weighs barely 220 pounds (one hundred kilograms), making him the second-lightest member of the makuuchi, after Mainoumi. Now twenty-nine, he is still very popular, but less threatening to the sanyaku than he was in the early 1990s.

Kaio of Tomozuna-beya is still just twenty-one and may have potential to reach at least ozeki.

IV

POWER AND TECHNIQUE

Takatoriki uses the technique *katasukashi* to overpower Konishiki, a rikishi twice his size.

Kimarite—Winning Techniques

There are seventy formal *kimarite*, or techniques recognized by the Sumo Association as ways to win matches. Many of these have actually fallen into disuse at this point, or become extremely rare. The techniques fall into three basic types—*tsukioshi*, pushing and thrusting tactics; *nagewaza*, or throws; and other general techniques, including many simple contests of leverage and power that make use of grips on the opponent's belt.

Sumo's techniques developed more than a thousand years ago, and lists of throws in the early Edo period still resemble many of the kimarite in use today.

In the last decades the average weight of makuuchi rikishi has risen by nearly forty-four pounds (twenty kilograms). Although this has tended to limit the techniques that are seen on a day-to-day basis, particularly versatile rikishi like Mainoumi continue to use some of the more unusual throws.

TSUKIOSHI—Pushes and Thrusts

1. ***Oshidashi***—One of the most common kimarite. The winner pushes his opponent out of the dohyo without gripping his mawashi.

2. ***Tsukidashi***—A barrage of thrusts that sends the loser out in a single charge.

3. ***Tsukiotoshi***—Similar to tsukidashi, except that the loser may be thrown down inside or outside the dohyo.

4. ***Oshitaoshi***—A simple push down.

5. ***Yorikiri***—The most common method of winning. The winner edges the opponent out, usually while holding onto his mawashi with one or both hands.

6. ***Yoritaoshi***—Similar to tsukidashi, except that the winner may force the opponent out of the dohyo, or cause him to fall down inside the ring, while still gripping his mawashi.

Oshidashi

Tsukidashi

Tsukiotoshi

Yorikiri

7. *Abisetaoshi*—Similar to yoritaoshi, except that the winner uses his own weight to force his opponent down inside the dohyo.

8. *Kimedashi*—The winner locks the opponent's arms beneath his own and, clamping them against his sides, forces the opponent out.

9. *Kimetaoshi*—Similar to kimedashi, but the loser is thrown down, inside or outside the ring, rather than simply being forced out.

10. *Okuridashi*—The winner, finding himself behind his opponent, takes advantage of this position to send the other out with a push on the back.

11. *Okuritaoshi*—A push on the back, in which the loser is thrown down.

12. *Waridashi*—The winner forces the opponent out, gripping his mawashi with one hand and pushing on his upper arms with the other.

NAGEWAZA—Throws (and Other Techniques)

13. *Uwatenage*—A common throw, in which the winner throws the opponent while gripping his mawashi from a position in which his own arm is uppermost.

14. *Shitatenage*—Another common throw, similar to uwatenage, except that the winner's arm is below (inside) that of the man being thrown.

15. *Kotenage*—The winner takes advantage of the opponent's outstretched arm (which is gripping the winner's mawashi). The winner bears down on the opponent's forearm, and throws him.

16. *Sukuinage*—Similar to uwatenage, but does not involve any grip on the opponent's mawashi.

17. *Uwatedashinage*—Similar to uwatenage, but the winner adds a pulling motion which brings his opponent down.

18. *Shitatedashinage*—Similar to shitatenage except that the winner adds a pulling motion while executing the throw.

19. *Koshinage*—The winner throws the opponent with a roll of the hips.

20. *Kubinage*—Usually a last resort. The winner throws an opponent down by means of an arm placed around his neck. Yokozuna Tochinishiki used this tactic against the massive Ouchiyama in May 1955, in one of the most famous bouts of the postwar period.

21. *Ipponzeoi*—Now extremely rare. The winner grips an opponent by the wrist and throws him over his shoulder. Must be seen to be believed.

22. *Nichonage*—Relatively rare. The winner trips the opponent by placing a leg around his from the front.

23. *Yaguranage*—Once fairly common, now rare. The winner wedges one leg between those of the opponent to upset his balance, and then twirls him around. The prewar yokozuna Tsunenohana and Akinoumi often used this technique effectively.

24. *Kakenage*—The winner trips the opponent, while also using the technique kotenage.

25. *Tsukaminage*—The winner grabs the back of the opponent's mawashi and throws him in a dramatic way.

26. *Uchigake*—The winner wraps one leg around one of the opponent's legs from the inside, and then throws him. The skillful ozeki Kotogahama frequently used this technique in the late fifties.

Abisetaoshi

Okuridashi

Uwatenage

Shitatenage

Kotenage

Sukuinage

Uwatedashinage

Shitatedashinage

Kubinage

Nichonage

Kakenage

Uchigake

27. *Sotogake*—Similar to uchigake, except that the winner wraps his leg around his opponent's from the outside.

28. *Chongake*—The winner kicks the opponent's ankle with his own ankle, then twirls him down.

29. *Kirikaeshi*—A defensive move, in which the winner deflects an attack and twists an opponent backwards.

30. *Kawazugake*—The winner, while standing side-by-side with the opponent, twists one foot around the other's leg, wraps one arm around his neck, grabs his arm with the other hand and, finally, trips him.

31. *Kekaeshi*—A combination of simultaneous thrusts and kicks.

32. *Ketaguri*—A combination of tripping the opponent and pulling him down.

33. *Mitokorozeme*—Very rare. The winner uses a combination of three different techniques at once.

34. *Watashikomi*—The winner takes his opponent out while grasping his thigh with one hand.

35. *Nimaigeri*—The winner delivers a kick to the outside of the opponent's leg, to upset his balance, then finishes him off with a throw.

36. *Komatasukui*—Gripping an opponent's inner thigh and pulling him down when he attempts to resist a throw.

37. *Sotokomata*—Similar to komatasukui, except the grip is on the outside of the opponent's thigh.

38. *Tsumatori*—Abruptly pulling on an opponent's ankle from the side and then forcing him face-down onto the ring.

39. *Omata*—Pulling, with the hand, on the opponent's far leg. Rare.

40. *Susotori*—Grabbing the ankle of an opponent who is already off-balance, and pressing it forward to bring him down.

41. *Susoharai*—A tripping technique that takes advantage of an opponent's having planted his two feet apart, sweeping the one further in front out from under him.

42. *Ashitori*—Using both hands to grab an opponent's leg and force him off-balance.

43. *Izori*—In this technique, the winner starts out low, gets the opponent more or less draped over his back and shoulders, then falls backward so that the opponent lands first. Extremely rare.

44. *Tasukizori*—Similar to izori. A rare shoulder throw.

45. *Sototasukizori*—Similar to izori and tasukizori.

46. *Shumokuzori*—Similar to the shoulder throws above, except the winner gets the opponent completely up over his shoulders before falling. Extremely rare.

47. *Kakezori*—Similar to izori. A rare sideways throw.

48. *Uttchari*—A last-ditch, defensive throw performed when the winner's feet are at the edge of the dohyo. Refers to turning the tables and throwing the opponent out instead. Once common, now less so as rikishi have grown heavier and less agile.

49. *Tottari*—Pulling an opponent over while grabbing his hand. Often used by ozeki Asahikuni in the 1970s.

50. *Tsukiotoshi*—Often used to deflect an opponent's attack, so that the opponent is thrust down onto the dohyo.

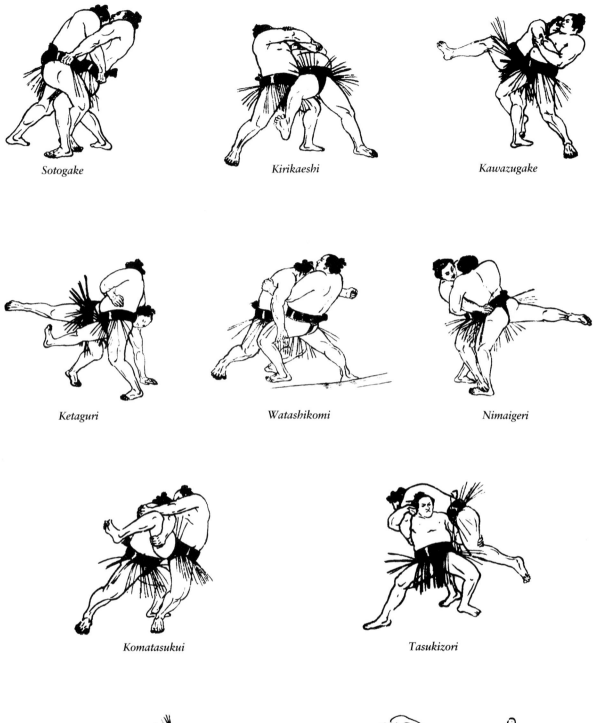

Sotogake

Kirikaeshi

Kawazugake

Ketaguri

Watashikomi

Nimaigeri

Komatasukui

Tasukizori

Uttchari

Tottari

51. *Makiotoshi*—A throw executed without any grip on the opponent's mawashi. The winning rikishi attains leverage by wrapping one arm around an opponent's neck and applying the other at some lower point.

52. *Sakatottari*—A defensive response to tottari, in which the winner deflects a tottari attack and uses tottari successfully on the opponent instead. Popular with sekiwake Tochiakagi in the late 1970s and early 1980s.

53. *Katasukashi*—Throwing an opponent down by grabbing the arm he is thrusting with.

54. *Shitatehineri*—The winner twists his opponent down after getting a grip on the mawashi with the back of the winner's forearm facing up.

55. *Amiuchi*—The winner wraps both arms around the opponent's arm, and twists him down, as if casting a fishing net.

56. *Yobimodoshi*—The winner first pulls the opponent in toward him to create some momentum, and then thrusts him away. Now rare. Frequently used by yokozuna Wakanohana I in the late fifties.

57. *Uwatehineri*—Similar to shitatehineri, except that the inside of the winner's forearm faces up.

58. *Zubuneri*—Twisting an opponent downward while holding onto his shoulders.

59. *Uchimuso*—Throwing an opponent down while applying force to the inside of his thigh.

60. *Sotomuso*—Throwing an opponent down by applying force to the inside of his knee.

61. *Harimanage*—The winner, at the edge of the dohyo, forces out an opponent who is coming to attack, by grabbing the back of his mawashi.

62. *Sabaori*—A bear-hug in which the winner forces the opponent onto his knees by bringing his own knees forward. Potentially dangerous and prohibited in amateur sumo below the high school level.

63. *Hikkake*—Side-stepping a thrusting opponent so that his own momentum carries him out.

64. *Kainahineri*—The winner upsets the opponent's balance by grabbing his arm with both hands and twisting it outward.

65. *Gashohineri*—The winner wraps his arms around the opponent's neck and then twists him down.

66. *Kubihineri*—The winner deflects an attack by putting his arm around an opponent's neck and twisting him down.

67. *Hatakikomi*—The winner uses the momentum of the tachi-ai, placing both hands on the opponent's head, back or shoulders and directing him down.

68. *Hikiotoshi*—Similar to hatakikomi, but here the winner uses a pulling motion to bring his opponent down.

69. *Tsuridashi*—The winner grabs the opponent's mawashi with both hands and lifts him out. Often used by Kirishima.

70. *Tsuriotoshi*—Similar to tsuridashi, except that the winner throws the lighter opponent down after lifting him up. Dangerous technique, and so not seen very often.

Makiotoshi *Katasukashi* *Amiuchi*

Sotomuso *Uchimuso*

Zubuneri

Sabaori

Kainahineri

Hatakikomi

Hikiotoshi

These photographs show a bout held in the mid-1920s at the second Ryogoku Kokugikan. Note the judge sitting on the ring proper. At the time, shinpan were positioned at each of the four corners, rather than ringside.

Both photos this page: Tomonohana defeating Tochinowaka with *sukuinage*.

Kotonowaka vanquishes an opponent with *uwatenage*.

Akebono wins against Musashimaru with *sukuinage*.

Tomoefuji uses *kotenage* against Terao.

Akinoshima thrusts opponent Naminohana out. *Oshidashi.*

Akebono's *tsukidashi* proves too much for Wakanohana.

Tochinowaka forces Wakanohana out and down with *yoritaoshi*.

Konishiki sends Jingaku out with *oshi-dashi*.

Terao uses a combination of *oshi-dashi* and the other man's momentum to send the much larger Kushimaumi out of the ring.

Naminohana forces Kushimaumi down and out, using *yoritaoshi*.

Asashio lifts Kirinji out, with *tsuridashi*.

Takanohana beats Kotonishiki with *hikiotoshi*.

Hatakikomi leaves Akinoshima splayed out on the ring.

Takatoriki tosses Higonoumi down, using *tsukiotoshi*.

Kotofuji uses *yorikiri*, probably the most common of all winning techniques, to ease Tochinowaka out of the ring.

A false start by Takanohana (left) against Musashimaru

Matta—False Starts

In an ideal tachi-ai, both rikishi place their hands briefly on the dohyo and then make a well-synchronized charge toward one another, which is followed by solid contact. The shikiri serves as psychological preparation for the tachi-ai and the entire bout; failure to perform a proper tachi-ai indicates that this warming-up process did not proceed smoothly, perhaps due to excessive tension or distraction.

In the years just preceding and during World War II, dominated by the great yokozuna Futabayama, most rikishi had outstanding shikiri and perfect tachi-ai. Futabayama himself was so confident that he was prepared to take on any opponent at any stage of the ritual stand-off before the bout. However, the fine tachi-ai of this generation of rikishi gradually disappeared as they retired. Beginning in the Tochi-Waka era of the 1950s, many rikishi began to make their charge practically from a standing position, or with just one hand barely touching the dohyo.

By the early 1980s the tachi-ai had deteriorated to such an alarming degree that then Sumo Association president Kasugano launched a campaign to restore a proper start. But bad habits were not easily corrected, and after Futagoyama Oyakata (the former yokozuna Wakanohana I) took over from Kasugano in 1988, he took the drastic step of fining rikishi for *matta*. In addition, another new rule has been implemented, stating that whenever a rikishi charges without first putting at least one hand down on the dohyo, the bout is to be halted by a signal from the judges to the referee.

Rikishi are not obliged to use the entire time allotted for the shikiri, nor is there any penalty if either should try to start the bout before time is up. Matta can only occur after the shinpan and gyoji have indicated that the match is to begin.

Makuuchi rikishi are fined one hundred thousand yen (or one thousand dollars) for false starts, while competitors in the juryo lose half that. Rikishi in the lower divisions have no regular salaries and hence are not fined, but may be reprimanded for repeated infractions.

The fine system has not completely eliminated matta, but certainly has helped reduce their number. In particular, the number of multiple false starts has fallen sharply. However, it will be extremely difficult to duplicate the precision of Futabayama's time, and eliminate matta altogether. After all, false starts date back hundreds of years.

Kinjite—Fouls

Sumo's rules—including its definition of fouls—are remarkably simple. Poking an opponent in the eye, twisting his fingers, kicking him in the abdomen, clamping one's hands over both his ears at the same time, pulling his hair, punching him with a closed fist, pulling him by the throat and grasping his *maemawashi* (the part of the mawashi that shields the genital region) are all prohibited. Should a rikishi use any of these tactics, the bout is immediately halted and the victim declared the winner.

The only *kinjite*, or foul, sometimes seen in the sport today—perhaps once or twice a decade—is hair-pulling. More often than not, a rikishi unthinkingly grabs an opponent by his mage while executing a throw.

On extremely rare occasions, a rikishi's mawashi may fall off. This has not occurred in the makuuchi or juryo during an official tournament since 1916. It is the gyoji's duty to tighten belts that start to come loose. The referee temporarily halts the bout, fixes the mawashi, then restores the two rikishi to precisely the positions they were in before. The gyoji would use his gunbai as a fig leaf to cover an exposed rikishi. But if a rikishi's mawashi were to fall off, he would automatically lose the bout.

Exhibitions of comical sumo known as *shokkiri* are performed at *hanazumo* (special exhibitions) and *jungyo* (regional exhibitions), but never during official tournaments. These include demonstrations of various fouls and other horseplay such as spitting chikaramizu on fellow rikishi or yanking off the gyoji's peaked cap to express displeasure with a decision.

Shokkiri performers tend to be the less promising rikishi ranked at the makushita or lower. On the other hand, yokozuna Tochinishiki performed these skits when he was ranked in the juryo and the lower maegashira, as did Dewanishiki, who would later reach sekiwake.

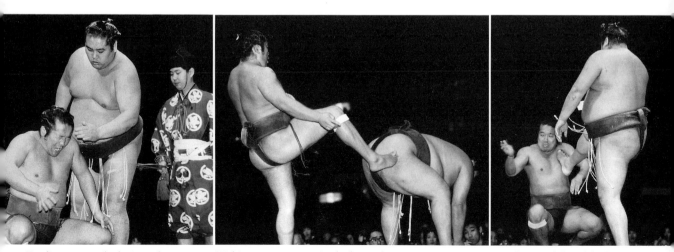

Fooling around during the *shokkiri*. Hair-pulling.

Kicking an opponent in the buttocks

Another prohibited kick, in the chest

Mitoizumi's customary cascades of salt never fail to please an audience.

V

DAILY LIFE

Heya—"Stables"

All rikishi, referees, ring announcers, elders and other sumo professionals belong to *heya* (pronounced "beya" in certain word combinations), which are often referred to in English as "sumo stables." The total number of heya rose to forty-five in the early 1990s, with each housing an average of about twenty rikishi.

Members of the same heya do not compete with each other during official tournaments. This exemption has worked to the advantage of Futagoyama-beya, which currently has three ozeki—Takanohana, Wakanohana and Takanonami—and seven other salaried rikishi. Yokozuna Akebono, on the other hand, faces everyone, since no one else in his heya is ranked at either the makuuchi or juryo.

Each heya belongs to a group known as an *ichimon*. Ichimon generally comprise an older heya and the newer ones that eventually branched from it. Ichimon have no official leaders, although the elder who operates the group's most powerful heya usually acts as the unofficial head. As of March 1994, sumo's ichimon consisted of the following heya:

Dewanoumi Ichimon—Dewanoumi, Musashigawa, Kasugano, Tamanoi, Irumagawa, Mihogaseki, Kitanoumi, Hatachiyama.

Tatsunami-Isegahama Ichimon—Tatsunami, Oshima, Isegahama, Asahiyama, Onaruto, Kise, Miyagino, Ajigawa, Tomozuna, Kumagatani, Takashima.

Nishonoseki Ichimon—Nishonoseki, Taiho, Sadogatake, Oguruma, Kataonami, Oshiogawa, Futagoyama, Araiso, Matsugane, Naruto, Minezaki, Magaki, Hanakago, Hanaregoma.

Tokitsukaze Ichimon—Tokitsukaze, Izutsu, Minato, Shikihide, Tatsutagawa, Isenoumi, Kagamiyama, Michinoku, Kabutoyama.

Takasago Ichimon—Takasago, Wakamatsu, Nakamura, Azumazeki, Kokonoe, Hakaku, Takadagawa.

Futagoyama-beya, sumo's largest heya, has over fifty rikishi, while the smallest have just two or three. All heya are headed by a shisho, the elder who owns and manages it. At present, less than half of all the sport's elders fall into this category. The others simply affiliate themselves with a heya, taking on coaching duties there.

Sumo heya developed in the Edo period, when professional sumo organizations were first established. Unmarried rikishi—including nearly all those ranked in the makushita and below—live in their heya, and even married rikishi stay in the temporary heya, usually within the grounds of temples or shrines, during the honbasho held away from Tokyo, in Osaka, Nagoya and Fukuoka.

Rikishi do much of their training in the heya, practicing between tournaments and on a reduced scale during honbasho. *Rengo-geiko*, or training sessions among the rikishi of an entire ichimon, are also frequently held just before official tournaments.

Training in the Heya

There are three traditional types of exercises used in heya, usually as preparation for *keiko*, or the practice matches against members of one's own heya that comprise much of a rikishi's training.

The rikishi performing *matawari* sits on the ground and plants his legs as far apart as they will go, then attempts to lower his chest to the ground. *Teppo* involves thrusting one's arms at a *teppo-bashira*, or wooden pillar, over and over again, in some cases more than a thousand times. In *shiko*, a rikishi raises one leg out to the side as high as it will go, then brings it back down, stamping his foot on the ground at the end of the motion.

This last exercise can be very difficult for rikishi who are especially obese. On the other hand, some rikishi have attracted attention with their superb shiko, namely the great yokozuna Chiyonofuji and the currently active ozeki Takanohana.

Rikishi practice these three traditional forms of exercise throughout their careers. Many retirees, including people who have left sumo altogether, still do shiko, teppo or matawari every day in order to keep in shape.

In recent years, many rikishi have supplemented their traditional training with bodybuilding regimens that include weight lifting and jogging. A few of the newer heya operated by younger oyakata even have weight rooms outfitted with state-of-the-art equipment.

Keiko—Practice Sessions at the Heya

Junior rikishi singing the heya song at the end of a keiko session; this is common practice at some heya, including Sadogatake-beya, shown here.

Lower-ranked rikishi practice every day, beginning at four or five o'clock in the morning. Members of the salaried ranks are not likely to join them until about eight A.M. The head of the heya generally supervises the training session, though in his absence another elder may take over this role. At about

eleven o'clock everyone breaks for the first meal of the day, and the rest of the rikishi's day is free.

Oyakata—Elders

Elders play a critical role in the sumo world, training active rikishi and managing the Sumo Association. The system of elders is almost as old as professional sumo—some of the 105 *toshiyori-kabu*, or names used by elders, date back to the early eighteenth century and before.

In the Edo period, virtually any rikishi or referee could become an elder. Toshiyori names were passed down from master to pupil, with the new elder paying no money but taking on responsibility for the livelihood of the aging former oyakata and/or his wife. During the Meiji period, the Tokyo Sumo Association decreed that only rikishi who had reached the makushita for at least one tournament would be eligible to become oyakata.

Current Sumo Association rules stipulate that a rikishi is eligible to become an oyakata only if he has spent twenty-five or more tournaments in the juryo or above, or twenty consecutive tournaments at this level. He also must buy or borrow a *myoseki*, one of the 105 historical names for oyakata (more commonly referred to as *toshiyori-kabu*, which literally means "the stock of an elder"). Since Japanese citizenship is also a requirement, foreigners must, before they can receive a myoseki, apply for and acquire citizenship, as have the two Hawaiians Takamiyama and Konishiki.

Though the term toshiyori-kabu does connote the acquisition of some form of security, the Sumo Kyokai does not officially recognize any monetary value as attaching to myoseki. Sumo Association rules prohibit both the transfer of myoseki to parties outside the sumo world and the use of retirement names as collateral for debts.

Former rikishi live longer now than they ever have before, with most surviving at least until the mandatory retirement age of sixty-five. This has created a much greater demand for toshiyori-kabu, to the extent that none are currently available. Elder names are now said to change hands for as much as 200–400 million yen (two–four million dollars).

Toshiyori-kabu can be borrowed or rented; borrowed names are known as *kari-kabu*. The actual owner retains the right to take back the myoseki at any time, and names are usually borrowed only for a few years. The practice allows the new retiree who was unable to obtain a name—whether because none was available, or he lacked sufficient funds—to stay in the sumo world until he is able to buy his own.

Gyoji are no longer permitted to become elders upon their retirement. However, the Sumo Kyokai recognizes the two chief referees as oyakata, and their names—Kimura Shonosuke and Shikimori Inosuke—as toshiyori-kabu (separate from the 105 used by retired rikishi).

Former yokozuna Taiho and Kitanoumi were granted *ichidai toshiyori*, or one-generation elder status, which means that they are elders, but may continue to use the name they had at the time of their retirement in their new capacity as oyakata. The Taiho and Kitanoumi elder names will cease to exist when the two former yokozuna retire from the Sumo Kyokai at sixty-five. The Sumo Kyokai grants ichidai toshiyori as a special honor to great former yokozuna, with Taiho the first to have been so honored. Chiyonofuji was also offered this status, but declined, as he had already made plans to take over the Kokonoe-beya and its attendant myoseki of Kokonoe.

All oyakata are eligible to operate their own heya, provided that they obtain the approval of the Sumo Kyokai, which is usually routinely granted. However, there are many more elders than heya, and more than half the current oyakata are attached to others' heya, where they serve as coaches.

The elders who manage heya lead especially busy lives. In addition to recruiting and training their own *deshi*, or the corps of rikishi under their charge, they also take part in the management of the Sumo Association. Some, like Kokonoe Oyakata (the former Chiyonofuji), also serve as judges.

The Sumo Kyokai pays a monthly allowance for food and utilities to all heya, based on the number of rikishi that each one houses, but the real key to financial security is having a strong *koen-kai*, an association of private and corporate sponsors that supports the heya.

The stablemaster's wife, or *okami-san*, also plays an essential role. She serves as surrogate mother to the young rikishi and helps out with cooking, relations with the koen-kai, correspondence and other important tasks.

The president and senior directors of the Sumo Association await Akebono's performance of the yokozuna dohyo-iri at the Grand Shrine in Ise.

Shindeshi—New Recruits

According to the rules of the Sumo Kyokai, any healthy male can become a rikishi if he is at least five foot six and three-quarter inches (1.73 meters) tall and weighs over 165 pounds (seventy-five kilograms). Those who have graduated from university and participated in collegiate sumo may be up to twenty-five years of age, while all others must be under twenty-two. Foreigners must have two Japanese guarantors and a valid visa and alien registration card. All potential rikishi, referees and ring announcers must have completed their compulsory education, which in Japan consists of six years of elementary and three years of junior high school.

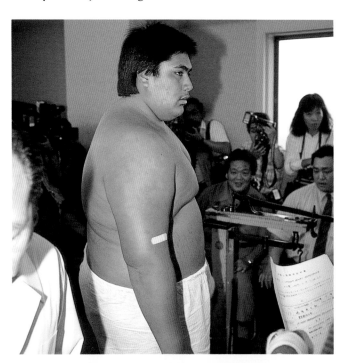

A new recruit undergoes the physical exam he must pass before being allowed to take part in a tournament.

Classroom instruction at the Sumo Training School

The majority of new rikishi are recruited in March, just after the end of the school year. Most will have just finished junior high. More than eighty-seven percent of Japan's junior high school graduates at least begin the next level of their education, but in sumo an early start is advantageous for advancement.

While some would-be entrants to the sport approach an oyakata directly, many others are scouted. Often at least one parent is opposed to the son's taking up sumo as a career, which means that the oyakata who hopes to build a strong heya needs to have, among other abilities, good persuasive skills.

New recruits undergo a *shindeshi kensa*, or physical examination for new recruits, just prior to the first honbasho held after they join the heya. The exam sets no maximum limit on height or weight, but does impose a minimum. Those who fail the physical for any reason may take it again prior to the next basho.

Rikishi who pass are eligible to participate at the *maezumo* ("pre-sumo") level, an unranked category in which they face only other newcomers. All those who compete are automatically promoted to the jonokuchi for the next tournament.

New rikishi are presented to the audience in a special ceremony known as the *shussei hiro*. Each young recruit wears a keshomawashi borrowed from one of the senior rikishi in his heya or from his oyakata, and is introduced by name on the dohyo during a brief intermission just before the start of the makushita bouts.

All new rikishi are required to attend the Sumo Kyoshu-jo, or Sumo Training School, in the Kokugikan for six months after they pass the physical exam. Here basic techniques are taught, in addition to classroom instruction in subjects like sports medicine, calligraphy and sumo history.

New recruits are introduced to the audience in a ceremony known as the *shussei hiro*.

Jungyo—Regional Tours

Regional tours and exhibitions of sumo (*jungyo*) date back to the earliest days of professional sumo. In the Tokugawa period, rikishi competed in major tournaments in Edo, Osaka and Kyoto, then performed jungyo at numerous towns lying between those cities. The three-hundred-mile journey from Edo and on to Osaka and Kyoto took weeks to complete in the days before public transportation was developed, and staging jungyo along the way helped generate operating funds and keep the rikishi in shape.

By the 1870s and 1880s, jungyo had reached every corner of the four main islands of Japan. Some held in more remote areas would center only on a given heya, or perhaps a group of heya, while exhibitions known as *daigappei*, featuring all the prominent rikishi, tended to be held in urban areas.

From the turn of the century through the early 1940s, when honbasho were held only twice a year, in January and May, marathon jungyo would sometimes tour not only the Japanese islands, but also Sakhalin, Korea and Manchuria. The summer exhibitions would typically move from the Kanto area to Niigata, then cross the Japan Sea by ship to Korea, where matches would be staged in cities such as Pusan, Seoul and Pyongyang. The rikishi would then cross the Yalu River and enter Manchuria early in July. They would go as far north as the city of Harbin in Manchuria before returning to Tokyo via Sakhalin, Hokkaido and the Tohoku region.

The present jungyo schedule evolved in the 1950s, when the system of holding six tournaments per year was introduced. Regional tours are now held after the March, July, September and November tournaments.

The March jungyo centers on the Kansai and Tokai regions, and always concludes with a free performance at Yasukuni Shrine in Tokyo in late April. The summer exhibition, which follows the Nagoya Basho held in July, is concentrated in Tohoku and Hokkaido, and lasts longest, generally extending over the full month from late July to late August. The autumn jungyo covers the Tokai, Kinki, Chugoku and Shikoku regions, and is held for about three weeks in October. The Kyushu jungyo also lasts for about three weeks, in

Daishoho signs an autograph for a fan during a spring regional tour.

Akebono and other members of the Azumazeki-beya pose after a practice session, with a kindergarten class and their teacher.

December, and takes the rikishi around the southernmost island of Kyushu.

Until the 1960s, virtually all jungyo were held outdoors, necessitating delays or even cancellation in the event of rain. Nowadays, most exhibitions are held in local gymnasiums, with which even the smaller towns are now equipped. Though outdoor jungyo have a charm of their own, moving them indoors has boosted revenues.

Jungyo are now all daigappei-style, and feature about one-fourth of the active rikishi, specifically those ranked in the juryo or higher and their tsukebito. The jungyo begin early in the morning, with training bouts (*keiko*) between rikishi of every division. Since training bouts are held in ascending order of rank, the ozeki and yokozuna do not enter the ring until about nine or ten A.M. Keiko is followed by exhibition bouts involving all the participating rikishi. Intermissions are held for shokiri, *sumo jinku* (renditions of sumo songs by rikishi ranked at sandanme and makushita), performances of traditional taiko drumming by yobidashi and other forms of entertainment. The shikiri is shorter than that performed in tournaments, and the bouts, being unofficial, are not as tense. Rikishi of the same rank are matched against one another, with the same pairings generally continuing throughout the day. The final bouts between ozeki and yokozuna wrap up the program at about three-thirty or four in the afternoon.

Regional exhibitions require extensive preparation. An entire section of the Sumo Association is charged with their planning and management, and oyakata oversee the arrangements at each site. A local sponsor who will handle the ticket sales must also be found for all regional jungyo. A dohyo must be constructed at each site, even if the exhibition is only to last one day.

Rikishi travel between sites by train or bus. Jungyo can be quite gruelling, as a considerable distance separates some destinations, and most travelling is done after the end of a day's bouts. Rikishi and other personnel are housed, in the smaller towns, in *ryokan*, or traditional Japanese inns. In larger towns and cities, the group will often stay in Western-style hotels.

While rikishi are scheduled to compete in honbasho only ninety days a year, jungyo take up another eighty days. The July–August jungyo is especially tiring, given the oppressive heat and humidity, but plays an essential role in toughening younger rikishi.

As a sign of respect, it is customary for the most senior member of a heya to offer the master a ladle of water as soon as he enters the practice area in the morning.

Junior members of the Sadogatake-beya finish up a practice session with a series of *shiko*, or leg lifts.

Former ozeki Kirishima practices against his *tsukebito*, or personal attendant, Nohira, during a regional tour.

Tochinowaka doing a set of push-ups

Kirishima limbering up with the exercise known as *matawari*

Akebono warms up under the watchful eye of his master, Azumazeki.

Daishoho (left) uses the opportunity of a regional tour to get in some rare practice with Mainoumi, who is a member of a different heya.

Futagoyama (the former ozeki Takanohana) gives some advice to his son and deshi Wakanohana during a regional tour held in Kyoto.

Akebono's master gives him some advice during a regional tour.

Yusho and Sansho—The Championship and Other Prizes

A single rikishi wins the *yusho*, or championship, in each division from the jonokuchi upward. The individual yusho system was formally established relatively late, in 1909, but is what gives tournaments much of their excitement today.

If a single rikishi has a win-loss record superior to everyone else's in his division, he is automatically declared the yusho winner. If two or more contestants achieve the same number of wins, a play-off is immediately held, consisting of either a single elimination match or a series of bouts, depending upon the number of rikishi involved (to win, one must beat everyone else who advances to the play-off). These matches offer the only opportunity for rikishi from the same heya to square off during official tournaments. The makuuchi championship has been decided by a playoff between yokozuna from the same heya only once in recent years—in the dramatic match in July 1989 between the two yokozuna Chiyonofuji and Hokutoumi.

The makuuchi yusho winner receives a cash award from the Sumo Kyokai of ten million yen and the much coveted Tenno-shihai, or Emperor's Cup. The solid silver Tenno-shihai was introduced in 1926, a gift of then-Crown Prince Hirohito, who would later become the Emperor Showa. The other prewar sumo trophies were melted down late in World War II, and only the Tenno-

After his first tournament win in May 1992, Akebono accepts the Emperor's Cup from Sumo Association President Dewanoumi.

Winners of the three *sansho* (smaller prizes awarded in addition to the championship) in the March 1993 tournament. From left to right: Kyokudozan, Wakanohana, Wakashoyo.

shihai was spared, since it was directly associated with the Emperor and had become one of sumo's symbols. Thus the Tenno-shihai awarded today is the same cup that the great Futabayama once held.

The winner himself receives a smaller replica of the trophy, which he is free to keep.

The makuuchi winner is also handed many other trophies on the tournament's final day. The most important of these are the *yusho-ki*, or yusho flag, from the Sumo Association, and trophies from the prime minister, the Tokyo Municipal Government or the prefectural government in other cities, handed over personally by the governor, and awards from various embassies. The Czech prize comes with a generous supply of beer, and that of the United Arab Emirates with a year's supply of oil. Makuuchi yusho winners also receive a car and literally tons of rice, beef, mushrooms and other goods from commercial sponsors.

Three additional prizes are given to makuuchi rikishi ranking up through sekiwake: the Kantosho, or Fighting Spirit Prize, the Shukunsho, or Outstanding Performance Award, and the Ginosho, or Technique Prize. Newspaper reporters make the nominations. Each award is worth two million yen.

Senshuraku—The Final Day of a Tournament

A honbasho's last day closes with the awards ceremony, in which the Tenno-shihai and other trophies are presented to the victor on the dohyo. The three additional sansho prizes are given out next, and the day concludes with a welcoming ceremony, known as the *teuchi-shiki,* for new rikishi who competed for the first time in that tournament. The newcomers form a circle on the dohyo with a referee and the final judges of the day, pass around a cup of saké, clap together the pairs of wooden clogs they are carrying and file out of the dohyo. Until the early 1980s, new recruits would toss one of the judges up in the air, much like a baseball team that had won a pennant or series.

The winner of the makuuchi championship poses with some of his supporters in the changing room, or *shitaku-beya*, then dons a formal kimono for the parade held in his honor. The winner leaves the site of the tournament in an open car, often with crowds lining the streets all the way to his heya.

Each heya holds an *uchiage*, a party to commemorate the end of the tour-

Konishiki's victory parade after he won the spring tournament in Osaka, March 1992

nament, on the night of the senshuraku. This celebration includes, in addition to all the rikishi and heya personnel, members of the heya's koen-kai and other guests. These parties were traditionally held at the heya itself, but in recent years most have been held at Western-style hotels, in order to accommodate the growing numbers of fans.

Rikishi generally take a week's holiday after each basho ends, though in some cases an exhibition tournament may be scheduled for the following weekend. The new banzuke is formulated at a meeting of the judging committee held three days after the end of the tournament. Promotions to juryo, ozeki and yokozuna are announced immediately.

When a candidate is being considered for promotion to yokozuna, the Yokozuna Shingi-iinkai, or Yokozuna Deliberation Council—composed of prominent people from various fields nominated by the Sumo Kyokai—meets and makes a recommendation to accept or reject the proposed promotion. The Sumo Association's board of directors is free to accept or overrule this decision, though in most cases it respects the council's wishes.

When a decision is made to promote a rikishi to either ozeki or yokozuna, two oyakata act as messengers, travelling to the rikishi's heya to notify him officially of the decision. The new ozeki or yokozuna, dressed in formal kimono, greets the elders with a few words of thanks, and pledges to do his

Wakanohana receives notice of his promotion to ozeki in July 1993. Flanking him are the father and mother he invariably addresses as his "master" and "master's wife."

best. The following day, the new yokozuna holds a *tsuna-uchi*, the ceremony in which his first ceremonial *tsuna*—the white, rope-like belt worn only by holders of the highest rank—is actually made. Then he practices the yokozuna dohyo-iri, coached by a retired yokozuna. The formal promotion ceremony and first official ring-entering ceremony are usually held a day later.

Hanazono—Special Exhibition Tournaments

Hanazumo, or special exhibition tournaments, are usually held after Tokyo tournaments, in January, May and September. One-day tournaments held to commemorate the retirement of rikishi ranked in the makuuchi are called *intai-zumo*. Other such performances are usually sponsored by television stations, sometimes with part of the proceeds going to charity.

Intai-zumo: The Ceremony Marking a Rikishi's Retirement

The *danpatsu-shiki*, a ceremony in which the topknot of a rikishi retiring from sumo is cut, is the highlight of an intai-zumo. If the retiree is a yokozuna, he performs the ring-entering ceremony for the last time, flanked by two current yokozuna. If no one else holds that rank at the time of his retirement, he will have ozeki or other rikishi from his own heya serve as his attendants.

The danpatsu-shiki starts with a speech given by the head of the retiree's koen-kai (supporters' association), who is usually a businessman or politician. The koen-kai head and the rikishi then stand in the ring and bow in each of the four directions. This ritual is followed by the hair-cutting itself. The retiree sits in a chair in the center of the dohyo while koen-kai members, friends and relatives take turns cutting one strand of hair each from the back of his elaborate topknot.

Active rikishi and elders take their turns cutting the oichomage at the end of the ceremony. The final cut is reserved for the retiree's shisho. This cut sym-

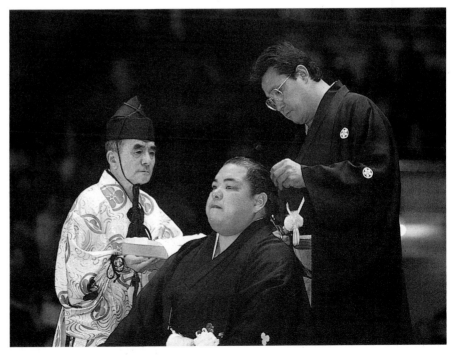

Here the elder makes the final ceremonial cut to the outgoing rikishi's topknot in the retirement ceremony known as the *danpatsu-shiki*.

bolizes the transformation from active competitor to elder, and is often an emotional moment. Some rikishi maintain their composure, but in many cases tears may run down a retiree's cheeks as he thinks back over a long and dramatic career.

This ritual completed, the former rikishi bows to the audience in every direction together with the head of his heya, then goes backstage for a full haircut. He dresses in a new suit, or in some cases a tuxedo, and goes to give ceremonial thanks to the shop proprietors of the Sumo Service Company, which sells a significant part of the tickets to honbasho.

The danpatsu-shiki is followed by the makuuchi bouts, and finally by the bow-twirling ceremony. The day ends with a party to celebrate the retiree's new status as elder, often held in the great hall in the basement of the Kokugikan.

Tickets to intai-zumo are usually available from the retiree's heya or from the Sumo Service Company, while tickets to hanazumo sponsored by TV stations are sold through playguides. Tickets to hanazumo are also sold at the Kokugikan on the day of the exhibition.

Chanko—What the Rikishi Eat

In sumo parlance, the word *chanko* is equivalent to "food." The mainstay of the rikishi diet, a stew containing vegetables, seafood and meat, is known as *chankonabe*.

In the 1700s and 1800s, the diet of rikishi resembled that of upper-class samurai and merchants. With the exception of giants like Shakagatake, Tanikaze and Raiden, most early rikishi were somewhat taller than the average Japanese, but not necessarily excessively obese. Until the 1920s, rikishi tended to live slightly longer than the average Japanese.

Chankonabe did not develop until the turn of the twentieth century. However, it quickly became a staple in the sumo world. Rikishi have become progressively heavier since chankonabe was introduced, except for the period of their brief but drastic weight loss during and just after World War II, when food was scarce.

During the 1920s, two top-ranking rikishi of the time are shown eating dinner at a restaurant with members of their koen-kai.

Rikishi eating chanko outdoors
during a regional exhibition

Though the process of preparing chanko has been standardized, each heya has its own distinctive ingredients and flavor.

Rikishi traditionally eat no breakfast and have their first meal only after keiko is over, at lunchtime. Competitors in the makushita and below usually take turns, known as *chanko-ban*, in preparing the meal. Some senior lower-division rikishi are especially good at preparing chanko, and carefully supervise the preparation of the meal.

Chanko is prepared in large pots, the ingredients added after the water boils. Lower-division rikishi serve the heya's elders, guests and higher-ranking rikishi first, and eat the meat they prepared last. Chanko is served with rice and numerous side dishes and, ideally, is washed down with beer.

Both lunch and dinner are usually prepared at all heya, but not every meal consists of chanko. Other types of food are served as well, and many of the higher-ranking rikishi eat out at night.

Many retired rikishi who do not stay in sumo as oyakata operate chankonabe restaurants, which are scattered throughout Japan. The chankonabe at these restaurants is authentic, although the volume of ingredients is less than in that prepared at the heya.

Additional Information

Honbasho Six honbasho, or official tournaments, are held every year. These are as follows:

Hatsu Basho Held in January at the Ryogoku Kokugikan in Tokyo.

Haru Basho Held in Osaka in March at the Osaka Furitsu Taiiku Kaikan (Osaka Prefectural Gymnasium).

Natsu Basho Held in May at the Ryogoku Kokugikan in Tokyo.

Nagoya Basho Held in Nagoya in July at the Aichi-ken Taiiku-kan (Aichi Prefectural Gymnasium).

Aki Basho Held in September at the Ryogoku Kokugikan in Tokyo.

Kyushu Basho Held in Fukuoka in November at the Fukuoka Kokusai Center (Fukuoka International Center).

How to Get to the Kokugikan in Ryogoku

The Kokugikan is close to downtown Tokyo, one minute's walk from the central exit of the Sobu Railway Line at Ryogoku Station. The Sobu Line runs between Hachioji or Mitaka on the western outskirts of Tokyo and Chiba Prefecture to the east of the capital. Ryogoku is the third stop after Ochanomizu, in central Tokyo. A subway line to be completed in the late 1990s and running in a loop around the city will also have a stop at Ryogoku.

How to Purchase Sumo Tickets

Tickets for Tokyo tournaments go on sale about a month before the opening day. In recent years, with the explosive popularity of the Taka-Waka brothers and other young rikishi, sumo tickets have sold out on the day they become available. The Sumo Kyokai has now authorized the Pia ticket agency to sell the masu-seki (box seats located on the first floor) through a telephone reservation system. Anyone can place an order, the morning tickets go on sale, for a single box on a specific day. But tens of thousands of people call wishing to reserve these seats, and it may take several tournaments before one succeeds in getting a reservation.

The second-floor tickets are sold directly by the Sumo Kyokai at the Kokugikan that same day. Though they generally sell out in one or two days, those who line up before the gates open at nine A.M. will have a good chance of obtaining a ticket for the day of their choice.

The Sumo Association also sells a limited number of tojitsu-ken, or tickets sold on the day of the tournament itself. These are the cheapest tickets available, and are usually for general admission, or standing-room. They often sell out before eight or nine A.M. on weekends, and by eleven A.M. on weekdays.

Types and Prices of Sumo Tickets

FIRST-FLOOR SEATING

Masu-seki—(carpeted box seats for four persons; with cushions) (A) ¥9,500 x 4

Masu-seki—(box seats for four persons) (B) ¥8,500 x 4

Masu-seki—(box seats for four persons) (C) ¥7,500 x 4

Box-seki—(Western-style box seats for four persons with table) ¥8,500 x 4

SECOND-FLOOR SEATING

Isu-seki—(single seats) (A) ¥7,500

Isu-seki—(single seats) (B) ¥5,000

Isu-seki—(single seats) (C) ¥2,300

Isu-seki jiyu-seki—(unreserved seats) ¥1,500 (adults), ¥500 (children)

How to Visit a Sumo Heya

Many sumo heya are open to the ordinary fan, especially during the periods before the start of a tournament. It is best to telephone first and ask whether it would be possible to watch keiko (a training session) on a given day. If one follows proper etiquette, it is also permissible to visit some heya without advance notice.

Sumo fans are expected to observe standard etiquette when they visit a heya to watch a training session. One should show respect to the oyakata by bowing in his direction when entering and leaving. People watching are expected to refrain from conversation, if possible, or at least keep it to a whisper. Eating and drinking are strictly prohibited, as they are in the suna-kaburi, or the single seats closest to the dohyo in honbasho and jungyo. An exception is the green tea that some heya may offer to guests who come to watch a practice session. Flash photography is not allowed (without special permission), as it may distract the rikishi.

The Media and Sumo

■ MAGAZINES

Sumo—Published monthly by Baseball Magazine Co., Ltd., since 1952. *Sumo* is the official magazine of the Sumo Kyokai, though it is published through a commercial publishing company. Price: ¥700. Available at most bookstores in Japan.

Ozumo—Published monthly by the Yomiuri Shinbun (one of Japan's largest daily newspapers) since 1954. Price: ¥700. Available at most bookstores in Japan.

Ozumo Tokushu—Published by NHK prior to each of the six annual honbasho, since 1975. Price: ¥600. Available at most bookstores in Japan.

Van Van Sumo Kai—A supplementary, small-format monthly published by Baseball Magazine. Price: ¥450. Available at most bookstores in Japan.

Sumo World—Published prior to every honbasho since 1973, *Sumo World* is the only English-language sumo magazine. Available at most bookstores in Japan dealing in English-language publications. Subscriptions available worldwide. Price: ¥650.

■ TELEVISION BROADCASTS

NHK—NHK has broadcast all honbasho live since May 1953. On weekdays, the regular television broadcast begins at 3:10 p.m., with the juryo-level matches, and ends at six p.m. (or later, if necessary). The NHK satellite broadcast in Japan begins at one o'clock in the afternoon on weekdays, with the sandanme-level, and at ten o'clock in the morning, or sometimes from the first jonokuchi bout, on the opening day of each tournament. In the early years of television in Japan, many of the private channels also broadcast all honbasho live. However, they found it difficult to provide distinctive enough coverage to draw larger audiences than their competitors, and all had withdrawn by 1966. Public-television station NHK has provided sole live coverage of honbasho since. The other channels sometimes sponsor unofficial tournaments, in February, June or October.

NHK Satellite—NHK's BS Sports Network now offers live satellite broadcasts of all honbasho to Japan, the U.S. and parts of Europe, with an English language commentary. England's Channel Four ran a popular taped sumo program from 1990–92. When that program was cancelled, NHK stepped in to fill the void in one of the areas outside Japan where sumo is most popular.

■ RADIO BROADCASTS

Live sumo radio broadcasts began in 1927. Initially many in the Sumo Association feared that live sumo broadcasts would reduce attendance at the Kokugikan, but the reverse soon proved to be true. Both NHK and Radio Kanto continue to provide live radio coverage of sumo in Japan.

SUMO HEYA

■ DEWANOUMI ICHIMON

Dewanoumi-beya

Dewanoumi-beya is headed by the former yokozuna Sadanoyama, who is also rijicho, or president, of the Nihon Sumo Kyokai. The present Dewanoumi-beya was established in the 1890s by former Maegashira Hitachiyama. Under the aegis of Hitachiyama's deshi, yokozuna Hitachiyama Taniemon, this heya became the most powerful in the sumo world. Dewanoumi-beya had more than one hundred rikishi during the Taisho and prewar Showa years, and so many sekitori that at any given time half of all those ranked in the makuuchi belonged to it. This heya's dominance faded with the rise of the great Futabayama (from the Tatsunami-beya) in the late 1930s. Though no longer the largest or most powerful heya, Dewanoumi-beya's prestige and traditions remain intact.

Musashigawa-beya

Musashigawa-beya was established by former yokozuna Mienoumi of Dewanoumi-beya in August 1981. Until that time, Dewanoumi-beya had had a policy of discouraging its retired rikishi from breaking away and establishing their own heya. Mienoumi, however, was granted independence in good standing with the parent heya, and has now developed two strong rikishi, Musashimaru and Musoyama.

Kasugano-beya

The present Kasugano-beya was established by former yokozuna Tochigiyama of Dewanoumi-beya upon his retirement in 1926. His deshi Tochinishiki reached yokozuna and won ten yusho between 1952 and 1960. Tochinoumi, one of Tochigiyama's last deshi, reached yokozuna and, later, upon Tochinishiki's death in 1990, succeeded as Kasugano Oyakata.

Tamanoi-beya

Tamanoi-beya was established in 1990 by former sekiwake Tochiazuma of the Kasugano-beya, winner of the makuuchi yusho in January 1972. In September 1993, Ohidake became the first member of the Tamanoi-beya to reach the juryo.

Irumagawa-beya

Former sekiwake Tochitsukasa achieved independence from Kasugano-beya in early 1993. A former collegiate rikishi, Tochitsukasa brought two other former college champions into his new heya in March 1993. By the end of the year, both had reached the upper makushita.

Mihogaseki-beya

Mihogaseki-beya has a long history dating back to the old Osaka sumo association. After it merged with Tokyo's association in 1926 to form the Dai-Nihon Sumo Kyokai, Mihogaseki-beya joined the Dewanoumi Ichimon. Ozeki Masuiyama I formally took over the heya upon his retirement from active competition in 1950. Though never a large heya, under Masuiyama I it produced several strong deshi. Kitanoumi became a great yokozuna, Hokutenyu held ozeki for seven years, and Masuiyama II (son of the oyakata) also reached ozeki. The younger Masuiyama (the present Mihogaseki) succeeded his father in 1984.

Kitanoumi-beya

Kitanoumi-beya was established in 1985, when former yokozuna Kitanoumi branched out from the Mihogaseki-beya. In recognition of his 24 yusho and outstanding record as a yokozuna, Kitanoumi was granted *ichidai toshiyori* (single-generation elder) status by the Sumo Kyokai. Kitanoumi-beya has became fairly large, but none of its deshi had risen above the juryo level at the time of writing.

Hatachiyama-beya

Hatachiyama-beya was launched in 1994 by former ozeki Hokutenyu, who branched out from Mihogaseki-beya, taking six young rikishi ranked at jonokuchi and jonidan with him.

■TATSUNAMI-ISEGAHAMA ICHIMON

Tatsunami-beya

The present Tatsunami Beya was established in 1915 by former komusubi Midorishima. Though the new heya was without its own dohyo for over a decade, Midorishima was one of the greatest shisho of all time, raising two great yokozuna, Futabayama and Haguroyama, and ozeki Nayoroiwa. The rise of Tatsunami-beya in the late 1930s put an end to Dewanoumi-beya's 30-year dominance of the sport. In 1952, Midorishima was succeeded by his son-in-law Haguroyama, who was then still active as a yokozuna (at the time there was no rule preventing an active rikishi from becoming an oyakata). Haguroyama also became a successful oyakata, raising ozeki Wakahaguro, sekiwake Tokitsuyama and Haguroyama (Annenyama), and komusubi Wakanami, all of whom won one tournament each. Haguroyama died in 1969 and was succeeded by the second Haguroyama (now Tatsunami), the current oyakata. Tatsunami raised a yokozuna, Futahaguro, who was forced to leave sumo without ever winning a yusho. This heya declined temporarily with Futahaguro's departure, but recently rebounded with the rise of four new sekitori—Daishoyama, Daishoho, Tatsuhikari and Tomonohana. Tatsunami-beya has been rebuilt twice, but still occupies the same site, close to Ryogoku Station, that it did in Futabayama's time.

Oshima-beya

Oshima-beya was established by the former ozeki Asahikuni of Tatsunami-beya in 1980. He has developed a strong heya and raised Asahifuji (now Ajigawa Oyakata) to yokozuna and Kyokudozan to komusubi.

Isegahama-beya

Though the Isegahama toshiyori name has a long history dating back to the Edo period, the present heya was established in 1929 by former sekiwake Kiyosegawa. Kiyosegawa raised yokozuna Terukuni, who held this rank from 1942–53. Terukuni took over the heya when he retired from active competition in 1953 and received the Isegahama name in 1961, when his mentor reached mandatory retirement age. Former ozeki Kiyokuni (the present Isegahama) succeeded Terukuni upon the latter's death in 1977 and continues to operate the heya. He lost his wife and children in an airplane crash in 1985, and a series of misfortunes have reduced the number of deshi in the heya to only four. The master is, however, starting to rebuild Isegahama-beya, and has raised one rikishi, Kiyonofuji, to the juryo level.

Asahiyama-beya

Asahiyama-beya was one of the most powerful heya of the old Osaka sumo world during the Meiji and Taisho periods. The heya declined after moving to Tokyo, but has continued to operate without interruption. The present oyakata, former komusubi Wakafutase, took over in 1975.

Onaruto-beya

Onaruto-beya was established by former sekiwake Kotetsuyama of Asahiyama-beya in 1975. Onaruto-beya had two sekitori in the 1980s. These were Itai, who rose to komusubi, and Ishinriki, who, though weighing only ninety kilograms, advanced as far as the juryo, and became a popular pro wrestler after leaving sumo.

Kise-beya

Kise-beya was established by former maegashira Katsuragawa of Isegahama-beya in 1957. He turned over the control of the heya to ex-maegashira Kiyonomori of Isegahama-beya, his son-in-law, in 1967. The current oyakata raised Aobayama to komusubi in 1979, but the heya has had no sekitori for more than nine years.

Miyagino-beya

Miyagino-beya dates back to the Meiji period. It was headed by the former yokozuna Otori from 1920 to 1956, and by former yokozuna Yoshibayama between 1960 and 1977. The present oyakata, ex-maegashira Chikubayama, took over in 1991. Miyagino-beya has no sekitori at present.

Ajigawa-beya

Ajigawa-beya was established by former sekiwake Mutsuarashi in 1979. It acquired its first sekitori, Kasugafuji, when it merged with Kasugayama-beya upon the retirement of the latter's oyakata in 1990. Because of his fragile health, Mutsuarashi turned the heya over to former yokozuna Asahifuji of Oshima-beya in 1993. Ajigawa-beya now has two sekitori—Kasugafuji in makuuchi and Mutsuhokkai in juryo.

Tomozuna-beya

Tomozuna-beya has a long and colorful history. It was home to the great yokozuna Tachiyama in the late Meiji and early Taisho years. After Tachiyama's retirement, the heya declined, and at one point ceased to exist. The present oyakata, former sekiwake Kaiki, took over in 1989. Tomozuna-beya's sole makuuchi rikishi, Kaio, has considerable potential.

Kumagatani-beya

Kumagatani-beya was established by the former maegashira Yoshinomine of Takashima-beya in 1978. The present oyakata has raised one sekitori, Yoshinobori, who showed early initial promise, but retired at the age of twenty-four in 1993, after he was diagnosed with diabetes.

Takashima-beya

The current Takashima-beya was established by former sekiwake Koboyama in 1993. Koboyama was the last sekitori raised in the old Takashima-beya, which closed down in 1983 when its oyakata, the former ozeki Mitsuneyama, suffered a stroke. Koboyama was then transferred to Kumagatani-beya for a time, but upon his retirement from the ring reopened his old heya. The new Takashima-beya has only one deshi.

▪ NISHONOSEKI ICHIMON

Nishonoseki-beya

Nishonoseki-beya was founded by the former sekiwake Kaizan at the start of the Taisho period. Kaizan was succeeded by his top deshi, yokozuna Tamanishiki. Tamanishiki died while an active rikishi, in 1938, after having developed a major heya with nearly one hundred deshi. Deshi of Tamanishiki later went on to establish Sadogatake-beya, Kataonami-beya and the original Hanakago-beya. Tamanishiki's successor was Tamanoumi, then a 26-year-old sekiwake. Tamanoumi turned over the mantle to yet another active rikishi, ozeki Saganohana, in 1951. Saganohana raised the great yokozuna Taiho, ozeki Daikirin and sekiwake Kongo. Kongo succeeded him and is the present oyakata. Nishonoseki-beya is now quite small, but has one makuuchi rikishi, Daizen.

Taiho-beya

Taiho-beya was established by former yokozuna Taiho of Nishonoseki-beya in 1971. He and former yokozuna Kitanoumi are currently sumo's only ichidai toshiyori (one-generation elder status). Taiho-beya has raised a sanyaku rikishi, Ozutsu, but has no sekitori at this time.

Sadogatake-beya

The current Sadogatake-beya (as distinct from the pre-war, now-defunct heya of the same name, which had no connection to this one) was opened by former komusubi Kotonishiki in 1955. The current oyakata, former yokozuna Kotozakura, took over in 1974, and has developed a large heya with nearly fifty rikishi, six of whom are sekitori, including Kotonishiki, Kotonowaka and Kotobeppu.

Oguruma-beya

Oguruma-beya was established by former ozeki Kotokaze of Sadogatake-beya in 1988, but still has no salaried rikishi.

Kataonami-beya

Kataonami-beya was established by former sekiwake Tamanoumi II in 1962. He raised the third Tamanoumi, who died while an active yokozuna in 1971, as well as sekiwake Tamanofuji, who succeeded as oyakata in 1987 and continues to hold the post today. Maegashira Tamakairiki is the heya's sole sekitori.

Oshiogawa-beya

Oshiogawa-beya was established by former ozeki Daikirin of Nishonoseki-beya in 1975. Daikirin had hoped to head the heya that had raised him, but when he failed to be nominated upon the death of Nishonoseki's oyakata in 1975, he broke away and formed his own heya. The former Daikirin (now Oshiogawa) has raised several strong makuuchi rikishi, including former sekiwake Aobajo and Masurao. The heya also houses Enazakura and Hitachiryu, both now in juryo.

Futagoyama-beya

Now sumo's largest and strongest heya, Futagoyama-beya was established by former yokozuna Wakanohana I in 1962. He was one of the greatest oyakata in history, raising yokozuna Wakanohana II and Takanosato, and ozeki Takanohana I (his younger brother; a twenty-two-year age difference separated them) and Wakashimazu. Upon turning sixty-five in 1993, he turned over all his rikishi to his brother, who was then head of Fujishima-beya. The former Takanohana I thus became oyakata of this new, amalgamated heya, which took the name Futagoyama-beya. At present it has over fifty rikishi, including a remarkable ten sekitori. Two are Wakanohana and Takanohana, the first brothers to be simultaneously ranked at ozeki, and the sons of the oyakata.

Araiso-beya

Araiso-beya, established by former komusubi Futagodake of Futagoyama-beya in 1993, has just two rikishi.

Matsugane-beya

Matsugane-beya was opened by former ozeki Wakashimazu of Futagoyama-beya in 1990, but still has no sekitori.

Naruto-beya

Naruto beya was founded by former yokozuna Takanosato in 1989. One of its members, Rikio, has already reached the juryo.

Minezaki-beya

Minezaki-beya was established in 1988 by former maegashira Misugiiso of Hanaregoma-beya.

Magaki-beya

Magaki-beya was established by former yokozuna Wakanohana II in 1983. Two of his deshi, Wakatosho and Yamanakayama, have reached the juryo, but the heya currently has no sekitori.

Hanakago-beya

The old Hanakago-beya of ex-maegashira Onoumi was powerful from the 1950s through the 1970s, housing yokozuna Wakanohana I and Wajima, and ozeki Kaiketsu. Wajima succeeded as oyakata, but was forced to transfer his deshi to Hanaregoma-beya, and leave sumo altogether in 1985 due to insolvency. Ex-sekiwake Daijuyama of Futagoyama-beya created a new Hanakago-beya in 1992. Hanakago-beya is the heya located furthest from the Kokugikan, and the first to be established in Yamanashi Prefecture.

Hanaregoma-beya

Hanaregoma-beya was established by former ozeki Kaiketsu of Hanakago-beya in 1980. Kaiketsu's deshi Onokuni reached yokozuna in 1987, but retired in 1991 with a mediocre record. Hanaregoma-beya merged with the remnants of the old Hanakago-beya of Onoumi in 1985.

■ TOKITSUKAZE ICHIMON

Tokitsukaze-beya

The current Tokitsukaze-beya was established as the Futabayama Dojo by then-still active yokozuna Futabayama, in 1941. Tokitsukaze-beya became one of sumo's largest heya in the 1950s and early 1960s, with Futabayama raising Kagamisato to yokozuna and Kitabayama, and Yutakayama to ozeki. Former ozeki Yutakayama, the current oyakata, succeeded in 1969. Maegashira Tokitsunada is now its heyagashira, or highest-ranking rikishi.

Izutsu-beya

Izutsu-beya was established in the Meiji period by former yokozuna Nishinoumi I of Takasago-beya. Izutsu-beya had a golden era in the Taisho and early Showa years, with yokozuna Nishinoumi II and Nishinoumi III, and ozeki Toyokuni. The present Izutsu Oyakata reestablished the heya in 1977, after it had broken into two segments in 1972 following the death of the old oyakata. Izutsu-beya was very strong in the eighties and early nineties, with six sekitori, including ozeki Kirishima, and the oyakata's sons, sekiwake Sakahoko and Terao. In 1992, Sakahoko retired, but the heya is still quite large and has promising rikishi in the makushita and lower ranks.

Minato-beya

Established by former komusubi Yutakayama of Tokitsukaze-beya in 1979. Minato-beya houses maegashira Minatofuji.

Shikihide-beya

Established by former komusubi Oshio of Tokitsukaze-beya in 1992. The heya is located in Ibaraki Prefecture, which makes it one of the most distant from Ryogoku.

Tatsutagawa-beya

Tatsutagawa-beya was launched by former yokozuna Kagamisato in 1971. Upon his retirement from the Sumo Kyokai in 1988 he was succeeded by the present oyakata, former sekiwake Aonosato. The heya has one sekitori, juryo-division Shikishima.

Isenoumi-beya

Isenoumi-beya is said to be the oldest heya, and has a virtually continuous history dating back to the middle of the eighteenth century, the earliest days of professional sumo. In 1961, Kashiwado became the heya's first yokozuna since Tanikaze's death in 1795. The present oyakata, former sekiwake Fujinokawa, took over in 1983, and raised Kitakachidoki, who is now the heya's only sekitori.

Kagamiyama-beya

Kagamiyama Beya was established by former yokozuna Kashiwado of Isenoumi-beya in 1970. Tagaryu became the first rikishi from the heya to win the makuuchi yusho in September 1984. The current sekitori are Kirinishiki and Chokairyu, both in juryo.

Michinoku-beya

Michinoku-beya was established by former maegashira Hoshikabuto of Izutsu-beya in 1974. The present oyakata, former maegashira Hoshiiwato, succeeded in 1991. Michinoku-beya is one of sumo's smaller heya, but has a juryo rikishi, Hoshiandesu, from Argentina. Another deshi, former juryo rikishi Hoshitango, also from Argentina, now competes in the makushita.

Kabutoyama-beya

Established by former maegashira Daiyu of Izutsu-beya in 1987. The oyakata's son is among the heya's rikishi.

■ TAKASAGO ICHIMON

Takasago-beya

The Takasago-beya is one of sumo's leading heya. It was established in 1883 by former maegashira Takamiyama. It has raised six yokozuna—Nishinoumi I, Konishiki, Minanogawa, Maedayama, Azumafuji, and Asashio. The present oyakata, former komusubi Fujinishiki, succeeded as shisho in 1988. Takasago-beya now has two makuuchi rikishi—maegashira Mitoizumi and Hawaiian-born former ozeki Konishiki.

Wakamatsu-beya

Wakamatsu-beya was established by former komusubi Imizugawa in the early years of the Showa period. The present oyakata, former ozeki Asashio of Takasago-beya, took control in 1989. Asashio's college connections have helped bring in several collegiate champions as deshi. Wakamatsu-beya's only sekitori is Asanowaka, now in juryo.

Nakamura-beya

Nakamura-beya was established by former sekiwake Fujizakura of Takasago-beya in 1986. It has yet to produce a sekitori.

Azumazeki-beya

Azumazeki-beya was established by former sekiwake Takamiyama of Takasago-beya in 1986. A Hawaiian, Takamiyama was the first non-Asian rikishi to become an oyakata. Yokozuna Akebono is the heyagashira.

Kokonoe-beya

Kokonoe-beya was established by former yokozuna Chiyonoyama in 1967, after he broke away from Dewanoumi-beya and joined the Takasago Ichimon. Kokonoe-beya has produced three yokozuna—Kitanofuji, Chiyonofuji and Hokutoumi. Former yokozuna Chiyonofuji took over as oyakata in 1992. With nearly forty deshi, Kokonoe-beya is one of the largest heya, but has just one sekitori, Tomoefuji.

Hakaku-beya

The newest of sumo's heya, Hakaku-beya was established by former yokozuna Hokutoumi of Kokonoe-beya in September 1993.

Takadagawa-beya

Takadagawa-beya was founded by former ozeki Maenoyama of Takasago-beya in 1974. Maegashira Kiraiho is the current heyagashira.

Glossary

arakida soil: soil taken from the banks of the Arakawa River in Saitama Prefecture, traditionally favored for use in forming the sumo ring because of its high clay content.

banzuke: the official sumo ranking sheet published before each of the six official tournaments held each year.

basho: tournaments of any kind; often used as a shortened form of the word *honbasho*, meaning official tournaments.

chanko (also *chankonabe*): the staple diet of rikishi and others in the sumo world, a stew containing vegetables, seafood and meat.

chikaragami: literally, "strength paper." Rikishi wipe their lips with these sheets of paper just before matches, after rinsing out their mouths with *chikaramizu*.

chikaramizu: literally, "strength water." Rikishi rinse out their mouths with this water just before matches.

chonmage: the relatively simple topknot worn by lower-ranking rikishi at all times, and by members of the higher ranks on informal occasions.

daigappei: regional tours (*jungyo*) featuring all the rikishi ranked at *jonidan* or higher.

danpatsu-shiki: that portion of the *intai-zumo*, or day marking the retirement of a salaried rikishi, in which his topknot is ceremonially cut off.

deshi: literally, "pupil" or "disciple." A member of a *heya*, or "stable," and thus coached by the elder who runs it.

dohyo: the sumo ring.

dohyo-iri: any of the ring-entering ceremonies performed by salaried rikishi (*sekitori*).

dohyo matsuri: a Shinto-style ceremony, held prior to each tournament, in which the ring is purified.

eboshi: the lacquered black hat worn during tournaments by *gyoji* (referees).

fumidawara: literally, "stepping-bales." Additional *tawara*, or rice-bales, sunk into the sides of the base of the ring and used as steps.

gunbai: literally, "war fan." The lacquered wooden board decorated with a long tassel, held by the *gyoji* (referees).

gyoji: sumo's referees.

hanazumo: special exhibition tournaments, usually sponsored by television stations and held in January, May and September. Other hanazumo are the one-day intai-zumo held to mark the retirement of salaried rikishi.

haridashi: "additional" rikishi from the *sanyaku* (sumo's four highest ranks). Officially, there are to be no more than two rikishi at each rank, but in fact there are often more. When this occurs, those who turned in the least impressive performances at the previous tournament are simply considered "additional," and listed on the part of the banzuke that juts out to either side in a T-shape.

heya: a so-called "stable," or group of rikishi training under a particular master (*shisho*). Alternatively, the place where this group lives and trains.

heyagashira: the highest-ranking rikishi within a heya.

higashi: the right-hand, or east, side of the banzuke, traditionally considered more prestigious than the west (*nishi*). Also, the left side of the ring, as viewed from the front (the north). Rikishi assigned to the banzuke's east also enter the ring from that side.

honbasho: official tournaments, held six times each year.

intai-zumo: one-day exhibition tournaments held at the Kokugikan to commemorate the retirement of salaried rikishi.

ichidai toshiyori: one-generation elder status conferred as an honor upon outstanding yokozuna. Rikishi who receive this status become elders under the names they used in the ring, rather than taking on one of the 105 recognized names used by elders. The name is called "one-generation" because it ceases to exist as an elder name when the man leaves the sumo world upon mandatory retirement at age sixty-five.

ichimon: a group of heya, often an older one and all those that eventually branched off from it.

jonidan: the rank just above jonokuchi. Sumo's largest rank, with about four hundred rikishi at present.

jonokuchi: the lowest division, to which new recruits are promoted in their second tournament.

jungyo: regional tours, during which exhibition matches are held.

juryo: the lowest-ranking salaried rikishi. The point at which rikishi, for the first time, receive their own attendants, a salary and the ceremonial apron called the *keshomawashi*.

juryo-kaku: qualification to referee juryo-level bouts.

kachikoshi: a winning record (greater number of wins than losses during a single tournament).

kanjin-sumo: the seventeenth-century charity tournaments that gradually developed into professional sumo.

kari-kabu: borrowed elder names. A salaried rikishi who retires without first obtaining an elder name (*toshiyori-kabu*) must leave the world of sumo forever. But if none of the 105 elder names is available, or the rikishi's funds are insufficient to purchase one when he wishes to retire, he may borrow a name for a short time.

keiko: practice sessions usually held in the heya, or during jungyo.

kensho: prize money awarded by sponsors to the winners of specific makuuchi bouts.

keshomawashi: the heavy, decorative aprons given to rikishi by their patrons and worn during the ring-entering ceremony.

kinboshi: an upset of a yokozuna by a maegashira.

kinjite: fouls, including punching, twisting an opponent's fingers, poking him in the eye, etc.

kimarite: the seventy techniques recognized by the Sumo Association as ways to win matches.

koen-kai: associations of fans who support a particular heya, helping to pay for daily upkeep, promotion, scouting, etc. Rikishi may also have their own koen-kai.

kokugi: literally, the national sport; sumo.

Kokugikan: the sumo arena in Tokyo's Ryogoku area.

komusubi: the rank above maegashira; lowest of the sanyaku ranks.

maegashira: the salaried rank just above juryo.

maezumo: unranked beginners.

mage: the topknots that were the most common hairstyle for men of the Edo period (1600–1867). Still worn by rikishi. See also *chonmage*, *oichomage*.

makekoshi: a losing record (greater number of losses than wins during a single tournament).

makuuchi: the top division of sumo ranks, comprising yokozuna, ozeki, sekiwake, komusubi and maegashira. (In other words, all salaried rikishi except the lowest-ranking of that group, those in the juryo.)

makuuchi dohyo-iri: the group ring-entering ceremony performed by all members of the makuuchi except any yokozuna. This ceremony occurs after all the juryo bouts have ended.

makuuchi-kaku: qualification to referee bouts between makuuchi-level bouts.

makushita: the highest of the unsalaried divisions. Few rikishi are promoted beyond this point.

makushita tsukedashi: the rank at the bottom of the makushita where special provision is made for qualified college sumo stars to begin their professional careers.

masu-seki: box seats at the Kokugikan.

matawari: a form of exercise used to limber up for training sessions. Sitting on the ground with his legs as far apart as possible, the rikishi tries to lower his chest to the ground.

matta: false starts.

mawashi: the belt, made of either silk or cotton, which rikishi wear during matches.

mizuhiki-maku: the curtain that hangs from the *yakata* and is decorated with the Sumo Association crest.

mono-ii: a conference among the judges which may be called in order to reconsider a referee's decision on a particularly close bout.

myoseki: the 105 names available to sumo elders, one of which a salaried rikishi must purchase or borrow before announcing his retirement if he is to remain in the sumo world as an elder.

nagewaza: techniques consisting of various kinds of throws.

Nihon Sumo Kyokai: Japan Sumo Association.

nishi: the rikishi listed on the left-hand, or west, side of the banzuke. Also, the right side of the ring, as viewed from the front (the north).

oichomage: the elaborate topknot worn by salaried rikishi during tournaments and on other formal occasions.

oyakata: elders. Retired rikishi who have reached the makuuchi division for at least one tournament, or spent twenty-five tournaments in juryo (or twenty consecutively) obtain an elder name and have Japanese citizenship are eligible to become elders. Elders either act as *shisho*—running their own heya—or coach at someone else's. All help manage the Sumo Association.

ozeki: the second-highest rank, below yokozuna.

rengo-geiko: large-scale training sessions involving all or most of the senior rikishi; alternatively, a practice session by all the heya belonging to a particular ichimon. In both cases, held just prior to tournaments.

rijicho: president of the Sumo Association.

rikishi: literally, "strong man." Often referred to in English as "sumo wrestlers."

sajiki-seki: alternative term for masu-seki, or box seats at the Kokugikan.

sandanme: the division just above jonidan. Less than half of all newcomers to the sport will advance beyond this rank.

sansho: three additional prizes, each of which is awarded, at tournament's end, to one rikishi ranked in the makuuchi. These are the Kantosho, or Fighting Spirit Prize, the Shukunsho, or Outstanding Performance Award and the Ginosho, or Technique Prize.

sanyaku: sumo's four highest ranks: komusubi, sekiwake, ozeki and yokozuna.

sashichigai: a decision by the judges to overturn a referee's call on a match, and declare the losing rikishi the winner.

sumai no sechi-e: large-scale sumo festivals held at the Imperial Palace as early as the eighth century.

seigen jikan ippai: words the referee says to the rikishi when the judge assigned to act as timekeeper (*tokeigakari*) gives the signal for the match to begin.

sekitori: salaried rikishi; in other words, those ranked at juryo or higher.

sekiwake: the third-highest rank, above komusubi.

senshuraku: the final day of a tournament.

shihon-bashira: the four pillars that traditionally supported the roof over the sumo ring. These pillars were done away with, and the roof suspended from the stadium ceiling, in 1952 in order to facilitate the television broadcasts of the sport which began the following year.

shikiri: an elaborate series of rituals performed by rikishi before each bout.

shikiri-sen: the starting lines from behind which rikishi make the initial charge, or *tachi-ai*, that opens each bout.

shiko: a basic form of exercise used to strengthen the legs and improve balance. The rikishi raises one leg out to the side as high as possible, then brings it back down with a stamp of his foot.

shikona: the ring names given to rikishi, which may be changed several times over the course of a career, especially in recognition of important promotions.

shimekomi: the silk mawashi worn by salaried rikishi during tournaments.

shindeshi: young rikishi; also, new recruits into a heya.

shin-deshi kensa: the physical examination which all rikishi must pass before participating in their first tournament.

shinitai: literally, "dead body." A ruling by the judges that one rikishi—though he has not touched the ground or gone out of the ring—is in a position from which he cannot possibly recover.

shinpan: sumo's judges.

shinpan bucho: head judge.

shinpan fukubucho: deputy head judge.

Shiranui-gata: one of two types of ring-entering ceremony performed by yokozuna.

shisho: an oyakata who owns and manages a heya. Less than half sumo's 105 elders fall into this category.

shitaku-beya: the changing room within a sumo stadium or other site of a tournament or exhibition.

shokkiri: comical display, including demonstrations of sumo fouls and other horseplay, performed by lower-ranking rikishi during regional tours (*jungyo*) and special exhibitions (*hanazumo*).

shozoku: the garment worn by referees, derived from Heian-period court dress.

shussei hiro: ceremony usually held on the eighth day of a tournament, in which each new recruit is introduced by name to the audience.

suna-kaburi: the single seats closest to the dohyo in official and exhibition tournaments.

tachi-ai: the initial charge rikishi make toward one another at the beginning of a bout.

tachimochi: a sword-bearer; one of the two attendants in the yokozuna dohyo-iri (see also *tsuyuharai*).

tategyoji: chief referees, whose number is limited to two and whose names are fixed as Kimura Shonosuke and Shikimori Inosuke. Special provision is also made for recognizing them as elders, though they are not former rikishi.

tawara: straw bales packed tightly with dirt and placed in a circle on the dohyo, forming the area inside which the match takes place.

teppo: a form of exercise useful for improving one's thrusting technique. The rikishi slaps at a wooden pillar over and over again.

teuchi-shiki: a welcoming ceremony for new recruits, held on the final day of each tournament. Those who entered sumo after the last tournament form a circle on the dohyo with the referee and judges and pass around a cup of saké.

tokei-gakari: timekeeper. One of the judges supervising each bout is assigned the role of timekeeper, and signals the referee when the rituals that precede each match are to end and the bout itself to begin.

tokoyama: sumo's hairdressers, who generally train for at least ten years before completely mastering the elaborate topknot worn during tournaments by salaried rikishi.

tokudawara: literally, "special rice-bale." One tawara set a few inches back from the circle at each of the cardi-

nal points, representing the only spots where a step outside the ring does not mean loss of the match.

torinaoshi: a rematch. The judges, after conferring on a particularly close outcome, may decide to order a rematch.

toshiyori: another name for oyakata, or elder.

toshiyori-kabu: alternative term for "elder name" (*myoseki*).

tsukebito: attendants. Younger, low-ranking rikishi may be assigned to serve as attendants, or personal assistants, to salaried rikishi or to referees qualified to judge juryo- or makuuchi-level bouts.

tsukioshi: techniques involving pushes or thrusts.

tsuna: the white, rope-like belt which the yokozuna wears for his individual dohyo-iri, and which symbolizes his rank.

tsuna-uchi: the ceremony in which a new yokozuna's first rope-like belt (*tsuna*) is actually made.

tsuyuharai: the second attendant who assists in the yokozuna dohyo-iri (see also *tachimochi*).

uchiage: a party held by each heya on the final night of the tournament.

Unryu-gata: one of the two types of ring-entering ceremony performed by yokozuna.

yakata: the Shinto-style roof (weighing many tons) suspended from the ceiling of the stadium, over the ring.

yobidashi: the ring announcer who calls the rikishi, by name, onto the dohyo. The yobidashi also carry the kensho banners, listing the names of the sponsors who have put up cash awards, before each bout begins.

yokozuna: sumo's highest rank, officially created in 1909. Often referred to in English as "grand champion."

Yokozuna Shingi-iinkai: the Yokozuna Deliberation Council, which decides whether or not to recommend the proposed promotion of a particular rikishi to the sport's highest rank.

yotsuzumo: techniques centering on various kinds of grips on the opponent's belt.

yumitori-shiki: a bow-twirling ceremony that closes each day of official and exhibition tournaments.

yusho: the championship of a tournament.

zensho yusho: a perfect record (no losses during a single tournament).